BATTLE
OF BRITAIN

BATTLE OF BRITAIN

NORMAN FRANKS

A Bison Book

First published in the USA for
K Mart Corporation,
Troy, Michigan 48084

Copyright © 1981 Bison Books Limited

Produced by
Bison Books Limited
4 Cromwell Place
London SW7

Library of Congress Catalog Card Number:
81-80457

ISBN 0-88365-546-2

Printed in Hong Kong

Page 1: Heinkel He 111s en route to
southern England.
Page 2–3: Hurricane in 111 Sqn
codings.
Page 4–5: Ian 'Widge' Gleed, DFC, of
87 Sqn, leading a Hurricane formation
from Exeter to Bibury in September
1940.

CONTENTS

1. THE BUILD UP

Below: Air Chief Marshal Sir Hugh C T Dowding, AOC in C, RAF fighter Command, during the battle of Britain.

Above: The distinctive outline of the Spitfire.

Britain was alone. The debris of Dunkirk had disappeared and those soldiers who were still in France were either dead or in prison camps. Western Europe was now under the heel of the German jackboot.

In an astonishingly short space of time France, Belgium and Holland had fallen to the German's lightning attack – their now famous Blitzkrieg tactic. In that time the British army had been forced out of France, the Royal Air Force had been overwhelmed, and Britain's allies had been defeated and forced to surrender their arms and their countries. In one month Hitler's forces, already victors in Poland and Norway, had achieved what the Kaiser's armies had failed to do in the four years between 1914–18.

Anyone standing on the south coast of England in mid-June 1940, and looking out across the English Channel toward France could feel tangibly that he and his country were alone. True, Britain still had her Commonwealth, but although some of its fighting men were in the Mother country, Canada, South Africa, Australia, New Zealand and so on were too far away to be of any real help. They could send more men and supplies but that was all. Britain was still alone and it was obvious to everyone that the Germans' next conquest must be the British Isles. In their way stood Air Chief Marshal Hugh Dowding, Commander in Chief of Britain's Fighter Command, and his fighter pilots.

Right: Hermann Wilhelm Goering, the 'supremo' of the Luftwaffe throughout its existence.
Far right: A Lockheed Hudson of Coastal Command approaching Dunkirk on a reconnaissance patrol.
Bottom: Part of the armada which rescued the BEF standing off Dunkirk.
Below: The forlorn remains of a Hawker Hurricane on Dunkirk beach, July 1940, epitomizing the utter defeat of Allied air forces in France during the Blitzkrieg.

Britain's natural defense was, and has always been, the Channel. Although the advent of the airplane had in one sense made Britain less of an island, an invading army had still to cross this watery barrier. That could only be achieved, again because of the airplane, if the invaders had mastery of the air.

To gain this mastery over the English Channel and southern England, the German Luftwaffe needed to defeat the Royal Air Force, or more especially, its Fighter Command. In mid-June 1940 Fighter Command was in poor shape by comparison with the attackers. Losses over Dunkirk and in the Battle of France had seen to that. It is said that one can prove anything with figures and various accounts of comparative strengths of the RAF and the Luftwaffe do differ.

The Luftwaffe, under the command of Hermann Wilhelm Goering, a former fighter pilot of World War I, had been building its strength for a number of years. By August 1938 it had nearly 3000 aircraft, and the total had increased to 3750 by the time Poland was attacked on 1 September 1939, which plunged the world into World War II. Despite losses sustained in Poland, and later over Norway in April 1940, the Luftwaffe mustered nearly 5000 aircraft by May 1940. Of this total 3900 were in the two Air Groups, *Luftflotte* 2 and *Luftflotte* 3, which were poised to lead the Blitzkrieg in the west.

Although the Air Forces of France, Belgium and Holland could field a large number of fighting aircraft, the RAF in France had only four squadrons of Hawker Hurricanes and two of Gloster Gladiator fighters in France during the period known as the 'Phony War' – September 1939–May 1940. When the Germans invaded France and the Low Countries on 10 May, re-inforcements of RAF aircraft were sent to France but in 10 days it was obvious that there was no stopping the German advance. The RAF gave a good account of itself in France, its pilots fighting themselves to a standstill. Yet finally those who survived had to be evacuated back to England. It was because of Hugh Dowding that Britain's fighter force had not been completely whittled away in the French campaign.

A scheme approved in 1935 promised Fighter Command a minimum of 53 squad-

Above left: Hurricane 1, N2479 of 56 Squadron at dispersal.

Left: Spitfire of Pilot Officer Colin Gray of 54 Squadron at Hornchurch in April 1940, armed, fuelled, and with trolley accumulator plugged in for immediate start up.

Left: Hurricane marked as the aircraft flown by Squadron Leader R R S Tuck, DSO, DFC, OC 257 Squadron in 1940–41.
Below: The sturdy Hurricane was the mainstay of RAF Fighter Command throughout the Battle of Britain.

rons by 1939 with which to defend the British Isles. In 1936, when Dowding became Commander in Chief, he only had 15 regular and three auxiliary squadrons. This was increased to only 24 regular and six auxiliary units by 1938 – and every one was equipped with a variety of outdated biplanes.

When the German offensive began on 10 May 1940, the RAF had 2750 front-line aircraft, of which just over 1000 were fighter types. In the first two days of the offensive four more fighter squadrons were sent across to France and on the 13th a further 32 Hurricanes and pilots flew over. Dowding had now been forced to commit around a third of his fighter force to France. Clearly this could not continue if he was to retain sufficient fighters to defend Britain.

He put his case forward forcibly at a Cabinet meeting, illustrating with graphs that if the present rate of attrition continued for a further two weeks the RAF would not have a single Hurricane left in France – or Britain! He followed this with his now famous and courageous letter to the Under Secretary of State for Air, setting out his fears and asking for the Air Ministry to

commit itself as to what it considered the level of strength needed to defend Britain. This in itself won him few friends in high places but it eventually did the trick. Shortly afterward came the order from Winston Churchill that no more fighters would leave the UK, whatever France's need.

The Royal Air Force eventually lost over 1000 airplanes in France and Norway, half of which were fighters. This represented two-thirds of all aircraft delivered to the RAF since the war began. Even more serious was the loss of so many valuable aircrew, both regular air force men and peacetime trainees. Their loss was not in vain for not only did they inflict considerable damage on the Luftwaffe, thereby reducing the number of aircraft which would eventually be used against Britain, but those who survived to return to Britain had gained immeasurable experience. The Dunkirk evacuation cost the RAF 100 fighters and about 80 pilots, leaving Fighter Command with roughly 470 serviceable aircraft by early June, of which just 330 were Hawker Hurricanes and Supermarine Spitfires. There were only 36 more in immediate reserve.

Left: Air Marshal Keith Park, the brilliant New Zealander who commanded the vital 11 Group, Fighter Command during the battle.
Bottom: Chain Home (CH) radar, 1940. The three towers at left are the transmitters; those at right are receivers.
Below: A Heinkel He III, one of the Luftwaffe's main bombers in 1940.

Right: Junkers 88 bombers played a relatively small part in the battle, but were to be used in a host of operational roles by the Luftwaffe throughout World War II.
Below right: The Messerschmitt Bf 109E, the only single-seat fighter type used by the Luftwaffe throughout the battle.

A month later, the first week in July, with both sides about ready to meet each other in deadly action, *Luftflotte* 2 and *Luftflotte* 3 numbered 2075 aircraft, of which 900 were fighters, 875 bombers and 300 dive bombers. *Luftflotte* 5, based in Norway, threatened the eastern side of England and Scotland and had 123 bombers and 34 twin-engined fighters. The RAF at this moment had just 46 fighter squadrons plus two equipped with Defiants (soon to be relegated to night fighting only) with four more squadrons in course of formation. The total number of aircraft was between 600–700 with 1253 pilots – 197 short of establishment. With this number, Fighter Command had to defend all of Britain, not just the south, although it was anticipated that the main assault would take place in the south.

Those in command viewed the coming battle with a good deal of foreboding. The task of defending Britain with such a small force against a victorious Luftwaffe was daunting. The pilots who would fight the battle viewed the coming struggle in a variety of ways. Some who had been in France felt utterly devastated at being on the losing end, a few even felt that Britain too must fall. Others were keen to hit back, to have another go. Many others, having tasted action above Dunkirk, were equally eager to have another crack at the Germans. Those pilots still to see action were, in the main, raring to go. Yet by far the majority believed they would prevail – defeat was unthinkable. This was perhaps a testament of youth, for most of Britain's fighter pilots were young. However young, they were the professionals, led by professionals. The wartime trainee pilots were not in evidence in any great number as yet. Whatever thoughts went through their minds, everyone was keen to 'get stuck in.' Yet within a few short weeks, those who

were still alive were physically and mentally exhausted and any excuse for a rest was gratefully taken. If rain or bad weather stopped flying it was a godsend. However, as July began each one of them stood ready.

One asset that the defenders had was Britain's advanced radar system, which was far in advance of the Germans' own development. When the battle started it gave the fighter pilots advanced warning of the approach of flying raiders, an estimate of their number and, with a degree of accuracy, their height. With help from the Observer Corps, 30,000 civilian volunteers, Britain had a good chance of knowing where the enemy was coming from and where it was heading.

Although as yet the air force had little chance to test its fighter defenses in nine months of war, the success in intercepting these few raiders that had made flights over Britain was encouraging. It was a practiced art and one that had been practiced often enough. This was due to the energies of the leader of Fighter Command, Hugh Dowding. His devotion to the concept of total defense of his country brought success although often his approach did not help his subsequent career. Even to his pilots he was an aloof figure – only later would they appreciate his great qualities of leadership.

Dowding's principal air leaders were the three Group Commanders whose squadrons would bear the brunt of the coming attack. All three had served in the air force in World War I. In the southeast of England was 11 Group, commanded by Air Vice-Marshal Keith Park, a New Zealander. North of the River Thames, covering most of Essex, Suffolk and Norfolk, was 12 Group, controlled by Air Vice-Marshal Trafford Leigh-Mallory. Air Vice-Marshal Sir Christopher Quintin Brand, a South African, commanded 10 Group in the southwest.

Opposing them was Reichsmarschal Hermann Goering and his three main air group commanders. *Luftflotte* 2 was led by Generalfeldmarschal Albrecht Kesselring, a soldier turned airman, while *Luftflotte* 3 was headed by Generalfeldmarschal Hugo Sperrle. Sperrle had commanded the Condor Legion during the Spanish Civil War, where the Germans had gained considerable experience fighting for General Franco's forces. *Luftflotte* 5 in Norway was under the command of Generaloberst Hans-Jurgen Stumpf, a former staff officer.

Historians have conveniently divided the Battle of Britain into five phases although at the time, to the ordinary fighter pilot, there seemed to be a general buildup from about 10 July, as the Luftwaffe stepped up its attacks, until October/November when they began to cease.

As July began, the RAF was still licking its wounds after the French and Dunkirk campaigns. Dowding's strength was far from 100 percent; several units had lost much of their equipment in France and were not fully operational. The Luftwaffe had moved rapidly into bases in Belgium, Holland and northern France, had been reinforced from Germany and now stood ready to take the offensive against Britain. By mid-July Luftwaffe strength was in the region of 2000 aircraft. Keith Park's 11 Group had just 190 or so day fighters and as it was the RAF's most vulnerable sector, the odds against it were considerable.

The RAF's main antagonists in the battle were Heinkel 111, Dornier 17 and Junkers 88 bombers, Junkers 87 'Stuka' dive bombers and Messerschmitt 109 and 110 fighters. All had had their successes in Poland, Norway and France, but over Britain their shortcomings soon became evident. The three bombers were all twin-engined craft with relatively short ranges when fully laden. In daylight raids they were vulnerable to fighter attacks and close escort by fighters proved essential as the battle progressed. The Ju 87, while success-

Below: The effect of eight Browning guns is well illustrated on this Dornier Do 17 (3Z + GS) of 8/KG77 (Obltn Gillios) which was hit by fighters, then downed by antiaircraft guns near Dover on 1 July 1940.

ful in the Blitzkrieg type of action when it could accurately blast a path for advancing ground troops, quickly proved extremely vulnerable in actions over southern England and had to be withdrawn from major involvement by mid-August. The Messerschmitt 109E single-seat fighter was a dangerous adversary for RAF pilots, but it was hampered by its short range. Often it had only a short time in the combat zone, usually measured in minutes, and its pilots were ever mindful of their fuel levels. The twin-engined, two-seat Me 110 was also dangerous but it had already proved vulner-

Above: A Hurricane landing.
Right: Bf 109E brought down in southeast England on 11 July 1940.

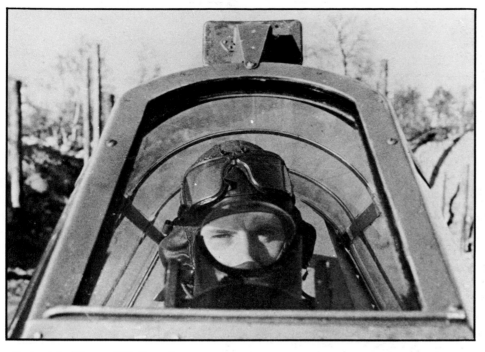

Above left: Pilots of 32 Squadron at Hawkinge, 31 July 1940. From left: R Smythe, J Procter, K Gillman, P Gardner, P Brothers, D Grice, A Eckford. All but Gillman, who was killed in action on 25 August 1940, survived the war. In background is Hurricane I, P3522, GZ-V.
Below left: Luftwaffe crews taking their meals. The order to attack can come at any moment.

Above: Flight Lieutenant A W A Bayne, DFC, of 17 Squadron in the cockpit of his Hurricane. Note rear-view mirror at top of canopy.
Below: One of the many AA units firing at night at Barry, near Cardiff.

able in combat over France. Pilots often had to resort to flying in defensive circles when under attack, thus leaving the bombers open to attacks by British fighters.

The Luftwaffe was organized principally for use as a direct support of an advancing land army. It was, therefore, totally unsuited for an offensive war involving distances such as France to Britain.

Both fighters and bombers were equipped with the 7.9mm machine gun, roughly equivalent to the RAF's Browning .303-inch machine gun, but in addition the Messerschmitts carried 20mm cannons which were much heavier hitting guns and could cause considerable damage to RAF Spitfires and Hurricanes. The RAF was experimenting with its own 20mm cannon but trials were not immediately successful.

The RAF's fighter tactics left much to be desired at this time. Squadrons flew in sections of three: a leader and two wing men. The problem was that although the leader was free to scan the sky for hostile aircraft, his two wing men were kept busier watching their leader and trying not to collide with him. Thus they were not totally concentrating on the sky around them. This rigid, inflexible formation took some time to change and even when more-discerning air fighters and leaders began to adopt a more open formation, and sections of four rather than three, others still continued in the old prewar formation. Even when proved effective there was no immediate directive from Fighter Command Headquarters to change to the new formation. Fortunately air fighters who had found over Dunkirk that flexibility made for more effective and less cumbersome attacks, put their theories into practice. Men whose names would soon be well known to the RAF and to the general public were emerging from the crowd: 'Sailor' Malan, Douglas Bader, Al Deere, Johnny Peel, Bob Tuck and Ginger Lacey.

German fighter pilots had discovered in Spain the advantages of a more open formation and flew in sections of four which split down into two-man elements once action was joined. In this way the leader was able to concentrate on an attack while his number two protected his tail. Already the Germans were producing ace pilots on their side of the Channel: Werner Mölders, Helmut Wick, Gunther Lützow, Walter Oesau, Rolf Pingel and Adolf Galland.

As Hitler hoped that Britain would soon request peace now that her European neighbors had been overrun, he had no wish to endanger a decision by attacking British towns and civilians. The opening phase of the battle was directed against Channel convoys and ports while the full German strength was being assembled in northern France. The German aims were to test Dowding's air defenses and to force him to use up his precious reserves.

On Wednesday 10 July 1940, the day that has become the official date of the commencement of the Battle of Britain, the first encounter of the day was made by a section of Spitfires from 66 Squadron based at Coltishall in 12 Group. Scrambled at 0440 hours, they intercepted a Dornier 17z of *Kampfgeschwader* 3 (KG3), 20 miles out to sea and shot it down. The successful pilots were Pilot Officers C A Cooke, J A P Studd and Sergeant F N Robertson.

The day's main activities centered around the Channel convoys which resulted in several air fights. At the end of the day, nine German aircraft had been shot down, with others damaged, for the loss of one RAF pilot who had collided with a Heinkel 111 over the sea. Six RAF fighters had been damaged.

The battles over the coastal convoys were vicious and costly to both sides. Several young, inexperienced pilots were lost chancing their arm against the Luftwaffe, some chasing Germans back toward France, only to be jumped by Messerschmitt 109s over the sea.

Over a convoy on the 12th, Dorniers and Heinkels of II/KG2 and III/KG53 were intercepted by Hurricanes of 17, 85, 151 and 242 Squadrons from Martlesham, Debden, Coltishall and North Weald. One pilot in 17 Squadron, Flying Officer Count M B Czernin, spotted 12 Heinkel 111s coming in fast from the east at 8000 feet. He immediately went into a climbing turn to the left, then, stick over and a kick on the left rudder and he was plunging down to attack. The Station Commander at North Weald, Wing Commander F V Beamish, flying with 151 Squadron, was also on hand. Attacking three Dorniers, he was:

'. . . met by heavy crossfire with much tracer. After a long burst at the left hand Dornier, his port engine blew up and stopped, his undercarriage dropped down and he broke away from the formation.'

Meanwhile, Czernin and one of his section, Pilot Officer D H W Hanson, had broken off the first action and followed Beamish's attack on the three Dorniers. They attacked the leading bomber and sent it into the sea. Its pilot was the Staffelkapitan of KG3, Hauptmann Machetski.

Later in the day three pilots of 74 Squadron took off to investigate a raid plotted 15 miles northeast of Margate. They saw anti-aircraft fire coming from a ship, exploding around a Heinkel 111. The section leader, Flight Lieutenant A G Malan DFC, opened fire from 300 yards and silenced the rear gunner, allowing his two wingmen to finish it off.

Sailor Malan was again in evidence on 28 July when he and his men tangled with Werner Mölder's JG51. No 74 Squadron was using Manston as a base and had been scrambled at 1350 hours when a raid had been reported approaching Dover. Malan's Spitfires went after the Messerschmitt escort, but the bombers turned away. The Spitfire pilots attacked the Me 109s; no less than three were destroyed and three others were damaged. One of those damaged was flown by Mölders himself. Malan reported the action:

'. . . turned on to their tails without being observed and led Red Section into the attack. Gave one enemy aircraft two-second bursts from 250 to 100 yards. He attempted no evasion tactics except a gentle right-hand turn and decreasing speed, by which I concluded he had at least had his controls hit (shot away). I then turned onto another 109 which had turned past my nose and I delivered three deflection bursts at 100 yards. He went down in a spiral.'

The squadrons that periodically used RAF Manston as a forward base were

Right: Flying Officer M B Czernin, DFC of 17 Squadron.
Above right: Pilots of 151 Squadron at North Weald, July 1940, including Wing Commander F V Beamish (fifth from left), and Squadron Leader E M Donaldson (forth from left), both of whom had several brothers in the RAF.
Far right: Spitfires of 66 Squadron get away from Coltishall in 'Vic' formation.
Below: Hurricanes of 56 Squadron at North Weald in July 1940.

constantly in the front line. Little wonder that this southeastern tip of England was soon called 'Hellfire Corner' by the pilots. It became liberally pitted with bomb craters as low-flying Me 109s were easily able to slip in to fly a strafing run over the base. Rochford (Southend) was another airfield and forward base similar to Manston and also used by squadrons from Hornchurch.

At Manston the pilots occupied a dispersal site on the far side of the airfield. They had some huts for both ground personnel and aircrew during readiness periods. This sometimes caused delays in bringing food and refreshments to dispersal as it was a long way from the domestic amenities of the camp. It was code named 'Charlie 3.' The typical routine for Manston, Rochford

(and some others) was: Readiness at Dawn. Takeoff straight away to fly a convoy patrol. Refuel and return to immediate readiness until mid- or late afternoon taking part in whatever sorties might come along. Then back to the parent station, remaining at Readiness until finally released at dusk.

No 65 Squadron used Rochford during one period. The conditions were somewhat primitive. Their Spitfires were parked into the wind while the pilots used an old civilian clubhouse as flight hut, restroom and eating place. There they would wait for the call for action. Parked outside the

clubhouse was a 15-hundredweight Bedford truck and a motorbike which was used to get to the aircraft in a hurry when the call came.

In the clubhouse was a single telephone which was answered by whoever was sitting nearest to it, while everyone else made for the door at top speed, aiming for the truck. 'Thumbs up' and away they went, leaving the chap on the phone to get the whole message then follow on the motorbike and pass on the message as they climbed away on takeoff. 'Thumbs down' stopped the panic and everyone settled

Above: A three-some Vic of 610 Squadron, AAF, on patrol, searching for the Luftwaffe.
Below right: A G 'Sailor' Malan of 74 'Tiger' Squadron who was recognized as possibly the finest fighter leader in the RAF, 1940–42.
Below: Wing Commander Brendan Finucane, DSO, DFC – 'Paddy' – who scored some 32 credited victories before his death in action in 1942.

down again.

One morning a young pilot named Paddy Finucane was nearest the phone and his sign sent everyone aboard the truck and away. As the pilots took to the air they looked down to see Finucane get onto the bike, fall off and try to climb back from the other side. With obvious signs of panic he jumped up and down as the others flew off without him. Upon landing it was discovered that Finucane could not ride a motorbike nor drive a car. They never let Finucane sit by the telephone after that.

The telephone became the center of attention in many crew rooms, dispersal huts and pilots' caravans over those summer months of 1940. The pilots would try to ignore its presence but as soon as it rang, their hearts missed a beat. Its message could send them racing to their waiting fighters, or it could be just an innocuous message, perhaps from the canteen, asking how many lunches were required, or the station commander wanting to speak to the commanding officer. The scenes at Manston and Rochford were repeated on a score or more fighter bases in southern England where the fighter pilots waited for the call for action.

As July gave way to August so too came the change of tactics by the Luftwaffe. The time of probing was at an end. If Hitler had any intention of invading Britain he had to attack in the summer, and before he did, Fighter Command had to be destroyed. On 19 July Hitler made his 'last appeal to reason' speech to the Reichstag – but he should have known Britain would in no way contemplate surrender. Hitler was confident of victory, for in his hands was the latest intelligence report comparing the Luftwaffe strength with that of the RAF. In its conclusion it showed that the Luftwaffe was clearly superior to the RAF in strength, equipment, training and command. In the event of intensive air warfare the Luftwaffe would be in a position to achieve a decisive effect in 1940 in order to support an invasion. What the report did not allow for was the dogged, stubborn attitude of the British in general, or the skilled determination of the pilots who stood in the way of German victory.

The first phase of the battle ended after the first week in August. In that phase the Luftwaffe lost nearly 200 aircraft, nearly twice as many as the Royal Air Force.

2. FIGHTER- VERSUS-FIGHTER

The second phase of the battle began on 8 August. The Luftwaffe now saw their task as mainly a fighter-versus-fighter conflict in order to destroy the British fighter force. The bombers which attacked British targets, mainly airfields, provided the bait to bring the Hurricanes and Spitfires to battle; then the Me 109 pilots could deal with them.

At the start of August there was a lull in Luftwaffe activity and it was clear to Dowding and to Keith Park that this had to mean that the enemy was regrouping ready for a massive all-out assault. Whether or not Hitler really meant to invade Britain, there can be little doubt that everyone in Britain did expect him to do so. Therefore, every pilot knew that destiny lay very much in his hands.

In the German Intelligence Appreciation of the RAF referred to above, the Luftwaffe underestimated the strength of the RAF fighters by half! This was to lead to various complications within the German High Command and the continuing shortcomings of Intelligence Reports led to much frustration among German aircrew who continued to meet strong resistance when they had been told that the RAF had been practically wiped out.

Dowding was a little more confident at this stage, for trained pilots were quickly making up the recent losses and he had now more than 1400 pilots; his only dilemma was that they lacked experience. Nearly 100 experienced regular squadron and flight commanders had been lost since May.

Of the many air actions which occurred on the 8th, two flown by Pilot Officer A N C Weir of 145 Squadron produced three victories. During the first part of the morning he shot down an Me 109 and a Ju 87. In a lunchtime battle he got another Me 109:

'Saw 110s in two groups five miles apart, flying in defensive circles low down. Three Hurricanes at 12,000 feet circled, wondering the best way to attack and asking for help. After ten minutes decided to dive when a 109 flew across in front of me – a decoy I thought. Pulled round to get on its tail and we flew round in circles till I was just gaining a position from which I could fire. He dived steeply and I fired from astern from 500 yards.'

Another pilot saw the Me 109 crash into the sea.

Goering had promised Hitler that his Luftwaffe would clear the sky of the RAF in readiness for invasion during early August. Now that his fliers had built up their strength, they were ready to go. His strength was 2250 serviceable aircraft between Cherbourg and Norway. Against this Dowding had 708 aircraft, an increase in the number he had started the battle with owing to the tremendous effort by aircraft factory workers.

As far as the Luftwaffe was concerned, the battle for Britain began on 8 August and Goering, head of the mightiest Air Force in the world, set 10 August as the date for his major assault, his *Adlertag* ('Eagle Day'). However, bad weather forced a postponement.

On the 11th heavy raids were directed against Portland, while a diversionary attack was mounted in the area of Dover. Three RAF Squadrons went up to engage the Dover attack while seven were scrambled to patrol Weymouth, near Portland. These found 150 German aircraft, Ju 88s and He 111s escorted by Me 109s and Me 110s. Huge dogfights began as the bombers pressed home attacks against the docks, oil tanks, gasworks and army barracks. At the end of the day the Germans had lost 38 aircraft but the RAF lost 32 precious fighters.

Above: Junkers Ju 88 of KG54 brought down by antiaircraft guns at Portland Bill during the Luftwaffe's raid on Weymouth on 11 August 1940. Note extended wing dive-brake slats.
Above left: Prominent among a galaxy of veteran German fighter pilots during the battle was Adolf Galland (in white jacket), who commanded JG 26 *Schlageter.*
Top: A Heinkel He III, victim of 'Sailor' Malan of 74 Squadron, erupts in flames.
Left: Messerschmitt Bf 109 bags a barrage balloon over Dover, August 1940. Such 'victories' counted as one-half when credited to Luftwaffe fighter pilots.

The next day was equally hard for the RAF defenders, as raids were directed against Portsmouth, radar stations and coastal airfields. The arithmetic was a little better. Some 31 Germans were shot down for 22 RAF fighters, although the Germans claimed 70 Spitfires and Hurricanes destroyed. These exaggerated claims did little to help German Intelligence reporting to the Luftwaffe High Command. The claims included the total destruction of one Spitfire squadron at Manston – 65 Squadron. They had been taxying out for takeoff when Dorniers of KG2 bombed the base, but most of them got off amid bomb bursts to join in the battle above.

RAF Hawkinge was also badly hit. Two hangars and the station workshops were destroyed and the stores building was damaged. Twenty-eight bomb craters pitted the airfield but it was operational next morning. The next morning was Eagle Day – 13 August.

The Germans were still not fully aware of how the operational structure of RAF Fighter Command worked, a fact borne out by the many attacks against airfields not even used by the defending fighter force. They were also unaware as to how the reporting chain from radar stations was coordinated. Their reconnaissance flight interpretation made some astonishing revelations, most of which were totally inaccurate and misleading.

Eagle Day saw heavy attacks on Eastchurch airfield in the morning and against Portland, Southampton and airfields in Hampshire and Kent during the afternoon. It was a massive effort; 1485 sorties were flown by the Luftwaffe crews, the highest number to date. B Flight of 65 Squadron scrambled from Manston at 1530 hours and off Dover they spotted 20 Me 109s. One of the pilots engaged was Pilot Officer B E Finucane:

'Saw three 109s flying in formation . . . and attacked number three, firing fairly long bursts from 300 to 75 yards. 109 burst into flames and dived into the clouds. I then spotted a lone 109 climbing up 400 yards ahead. Closed to 200 yards and gave it a burst. Drawing near could see the 109 had orange wing tips. 109 half rolled very slowly and seemed to shudder then slowly spin away. . . .'

Pilot Officer P C F 'Paddy' Stevenson of 74 Squadron was flying as Number Two to Sailor Malan and saw an Me 109 chase after his leader:

'He must have thought I was an Me 109 but when he suddenly dived away I followed him and gave a two-second deflection burst. The EA (enemy aircraft) lurched slightly and went into a vertical dive. I saw the EA dive straight into the sea 15 miles SE of Dover and disappear in a big splash.'

Stevenson climbed again and was about to engage more Me 109s when he was hit from behind. Looking back he saw a dozen Me 109s on his tail, half of whom seemed to be firing at him. His Spitfire was hit and he had to get out as he went into a dive:

'I pulled the hood back. I got my head out of the cockpit and the slipstream tore the rest of me clear out of the machine. My trouser leg and both shoes were torn off. I saw my machine crash into the sea a mile off Deal.'

The pilots of 609 Squadron got in among a formation of Ju 87s over Lyme Bay shortly after 1600 hours and shot down six of them without loss. Pilot Officer D M Crook, Number Three in Blue Section, saw several Me 109s pass right under his squadron:

'I immediately broke away and attacked one which was behind the rest. Fired a good burst from dead astern. He rocked violently and then turned over and burst into flames and crashed near Hardy's Monument behind Weymouth.'

Right: Out of ammunition and fuel, Hurricanes of 32 Squadron let down at Biggin Hill on 15 August 1940. Note airman with flag to guide aircraft through a network of bomb craters on the grass airfield.
Inset right: The parade ground at RAF Hemswell, Lincolnshire, receives a direct bomb hit on 27 August 1940.
Left: Junkers Ju 88, victim of the 13 August battles.
Above left: Messerschmitt Bf 110 at the receiving end of a Spitfire's guns.

Above: Airmen threading .303-inch ammunition belts into the wing boxes of a 610 Squadron, AAF Hurricane.
Above Left: Engine fitters testing the Merlin engine of a Hurricane. Note fabric-covered ports of the starboard wing's four-gun battery.

At the other end of the scale, the Hurricanes of 56 Squadron did not fare so well. They broke through some scattered cloud to meet between 12–20 Ju 88s, escorted by some 30 Me 109s with Me 110s above. Seeing the Hurricanes the Ju 88s began to jettison their bombs and turn over Canterbury – then the Me 110s came hurtling down and the air was full of twisting aircraft, Hurricanes, Me 110s and Me 109s. As one pilot put it:

'The 109s hurtle past and then up. Straight above are about 40 109s and one Hurricane. The whole sight is so commonplace and natural. Forty odd aircraft are wheeling aimlessly, slowly, like so many plovers on a windy day, yet it is a fight for life.'

Three Me 110s were claimed destroyed, but two Hurricanes went down in flames and their pilots were badly burned. Another also took to his parachute but was wounded, while a fourth crash landed at RAF Hawkinge. A fifth pilot hit an Me 110 but was blasted by another. He too left his crippled fighter, delayed deploying his parachute from 12,000–6000 feet in order to clear the battle area, and eventually landed in the sea two and a half miles from the beach, but successfully swam ashore.

At the end of this momentous day the statistics were better, 45 German aircraft brought down for the loss of just 13 RAF fighters. Ten of the pilots were saved

Below: Armorers working quickly to rearm a Spitfire of 19 Squadron at Duxford.

Above: Eric James Brindley Nicolson, VC, DFC, the only fighter pilot awarded a Victoria Cross during the war.
Right: H M Stephen, DSO, (left) and J C Mungo-Park, DFC of 74 'Tiger' Squadron, Summer 1940.

Lee-on-Solent and Brize Norton were all hit but only Tangmere was a fighter field. Flight Lieutenant R F Boyd of 602 Squadron based at Tangmere's satellite base at Westhampnett made what is probably the quickest kill of the battle. Scrambling when Tangmere was being bombed, he ran straight into a Ju 87, shot it down and was back on the ground in less than a minute after takeoff.

These raids cost the Germans a further 45 aircraft, the RAF losing 22 and eight pilots. One of these was the Hurricane flown by Flight Lieutenant J B Nicolson of 249 Squadron. He and his section became embroiled with German raiders over Southampton at 1245 hours. It was Nicolson's first taste of action. Following an abortive chase after three Ju 88s, he and his two wingmen were rejoining the main squadron formation when they were bounced by Me 109s. All three Hurricanes were hit; one pilot was forced to land at Boscombe, a second baled out only to have his parachute shredded by ground fire, sending him to his death. Nicolson's machine was set ablaze and he was wounded. He heard four big bangs as cannon shells from an attacking Me 109 hit home:

'The first shell tore through the hood over my cockpit and sent splinters into my left eye. One splinter I discovered later, nearly severed my eyelid. I couldn't see through that eye for blood. The second cannon shell struck my spare petrol tank and set it on fire. The third shell crashed into the cockpit and tore off my right trouser leg. The fourth shell struck the back of my left shoe. It shattered the heel of the shoe and made quite a mess of my left foot.

I was just thinking of jumping out when suddenly a Messerschmitt 110 whizzed under me and got right in my gun-sight. . . . I pressed the gun button for the Messerschmitt was in nice range; I plugged him first time and could see my tracer bullets entering the German machine.'

Despite the flames he continued to attack until he finally was forced to take to his parachute. Wounded and badly burned he survived to receive Fighter Command's only Victoria Cross of the war.

Hurricanes of 615 Squadron were in evidence during a raid near Brighton at 1615 hours. Pilot Officer J A P McClintock attacked one He 111 he found out of formation. He opened fire from 300 yards closing in to 50. The Heinkel's starboard engine began to pour out smoke, followed by flames, then it went down. Pilot Officer C R

Young attacked two others, one of which he left smoking. The second, hit by a long burst, went down into cloud and Young followed it. Coming out he fired again from 100 yards. The bomber levelled out at sea level, streaming smoke, but a third burst sent it crashing into the sea leaving a large green swirl on the water.

Flight Lieutenant P C Hughes, an Australian with 234 Squadron, shot down two Me 109s at around 1830 hours south of the Isle of Wight. He saw 50 Me 109s circling above him and led his section in a climbing attack:

'I fired a deflection shot at the nearest 109 . . . it caught fire and blew up. I felt a jolt and turned sharply and found another 109 on my tail. He immediately climbed away in front of me where I shot him behind the cockpit. He caught fire and crashed into the sea. Four Ju 87s went by, heading south. I closed to attack but as I fired my tailplane got shot through by a 109. My aircraft dived and my tabs were shot away.'

The next major assault against RAF airfields came on the 18th. Kenley, Biggin Hill, Croydon and West Malling were all attacked. Some 100 bombs fell on Kenley,

The day was another disaster for the Luftwaffe, 71 of their aircraft failed to get home. Twenty-seven RAF fighters and 10 pilots were lost. The 18th saw the death-knell of the Ju 87 over England, until late autumn at any rate. This made a total of 194 Luftwaffe aircraft lost between 15–18 August, with many more damaged.

Although the RAF was still suffering casualties it was nevertheless making its presence felt. Yet Keith Park was extremely conscious of the dangers his pilots were in and had to try and restrain their exuberance in engaging enemy fighters which in themselves posed no danger to Britain. His fighter strength had to damage the German bombers and stop them turning his fighter bases into rubble.

After the mammoth battles of the last few days there was a relative calm owing to bad weather between 19–23 August. The latter date ended the second phase of the battle which had cost the Luftwaffe in the region of 300 aircraft. The third phase began on the 24th. It was the crucial phase for Fighter Command – the Germans were after its blood – the RAF had to be destroyed.

Left: Cuthbert Orde sketch of Flight Lieutenant 'Willie' Rhodes-Moorhouse, DFC of 601 Squadron, AAF.
Below: Pilot Officer A N C Weir, DFC, of 145 Sqn, later killed in action.

Bottom: A victim of the clashes on 23 August, a Bf 110, goes on public display at Hendon Park.
Below: Max Aitken, DSO, DFC, son of Lord Beaverbrook, served in 601 Sqn.

destroying four Hurricanes, one Blenheim and three training types. Several hangars were destroyed and there were some personnel casualties. Kenley's 615 Squadron was attacked by Me 109s at high level. One pilot was lost, another baled out wounded and two more force landed, one being wounded.

Flying Officer F Gruska, a Polish pilot flying with 65 Squadron from Rochford, was reported missing at 1330 hours. His wrecked Spitfire with his body still in the cockpit was recovered from Stodmarsh near Canterbury, in July 1975 – 35 years later!

A massed Stuka attack on Ford and Thorney Island airfields was met by 152, 601, 602 and 234 Squadrons. Sixteen of the dive bombers were shot down, six more being damaged, two of which crashed at their base. Eight escorting Me 109s were also shot down but four Spitfires and two Hurricanes were lost.

Flying Officer W Rhodes-Moorhouse, son of the World War I VC winner, was a flight leader with 601 Squadron, although he often led the squadron in action. He got one of the Me 109s:

'There were two formations of Ju 87s, 20 machines in each, flying in close vic formation and stepped up in line astern was about 20 Me 109s above and to the sides. I gave the order for sections to form line astern and turning right I dived on the rear formation of Ju 87s making a head-on attack from the starboard bow. I saw no result from this attack. Passing quickly I became engaged with a lot of Me 109s at which I fired a number of short bursts . . . only one of these did I see crash as I had no time to follow or watch results of my attack.'

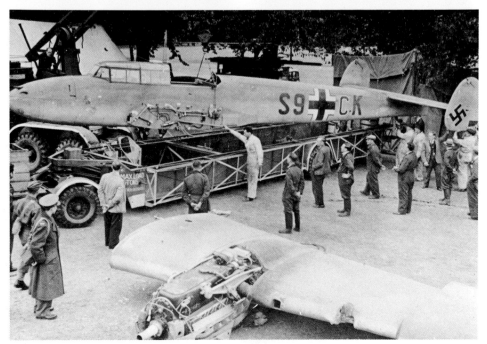

3. AIRFIELDS ATTACKED

The fighter pilots of the RAF were tiring. The previous weeks had been a hard slog. Pilots in the south of England had already been called to perform Herculean tasks almost daily. Readiness was at dawn – always at dawn. Readiness states varied from cockpit 'standby' of two minutes or readiness in the dispersal hut (or outside it in the sunshine) of five minutes. From time to time the squadron might be put down at 15 or 30 minutes availability, which gave the pilots time to go for a wash or bath or a hot meal.

Pilot Officer H A C Bird-Wilson, a member of 17 Squadron based at Debden for the first two phases of the battle, remembers those moments which began with the telephone ringing at dispersal. Most rings meant 'scramble,' excitement, acceleration of heart beats and a dash to the aircraft. On a dawn scramble it was known

Left: Men of 74 Squadron at their dispersal hut. At left Henryk Szcesny, DFC from Poland, with J C Mungo-Park, DFC (center).
Below left: Spitfire pilots of 610 Squadron, AAF relax between sorties at Biggin Hill.
Right: The Operations Room at HQ Fighter Command, RAF Bentley Priory, Middlesex, in 1940, with controllers and WAAF plotters around the central plot table.

for some pilots to scramble in their pajamas. Takeoffs from the grass airfield were usually in squadron strength of four sections of three Hurricanes, from two different corners of the airfield. At times 12 Hurricanes approached each other in the center of the airfield, lifting up over each other. Somehow they got away with it. The climb-out vector was always to the southeast to the left of London. Climbs were always made flat-out and with full throttle. Their ground controllers were superb and information was continually passed to the pilots, such as, enemy formation of 160 plus approaching the south coast at 12,000 feet, and above there are more bandits joining up with them – so climb harder!

It was a strange phenomenon, but many individual squadrons scrambled flew on their own. Each climbed to engage the enemy as just one unit, but hoped that somewhere near would be at least one other 12-man squadron. (Harold Bird-Wilson recalls this feeling vividly.) In contrast, Pilot Officer H M Stephen who flew with 74 Squadron, remembers being too damn scared of his legendary Commanding Officer, Sailor Malan, to think of anything else than to climb hard and get stuck into the Germans.

If squadrons engaged alone there would be 12 against 100 or more aircraft. As they fought as small units they had little idea of what the overall picture was. They took off, flew hard, fought hard and those who got back waited for the next call. They learned little of what was going on outside their immediate circle of action. They heard the news bulletins, of course, and read newspapers, but it did not mean that much to them. Even their squadron commanders knew little more and they certainly did not know about the whole picture of the battle. The individual pilot merely lived from dawn readiness until released at dusk, and with dawn at 0330 hours or so, it was a long day. Little wonder they slept where they sat or lay between flights.

At their dispersal points the pilots had certain creature comforts. Some had easy chairs, others had camp beds pulled out into the sunshine. There was the inevitable record player and sometimes a radio. Twelve men would sit in the warm sun in a variety of uniform or flying clothing, Mae West life jackets on. Within a short distance stood their aircraft, trolley starter accumu-

lator plugged in. Each fighter's ground crew sitting or lying nearby was ready to start the machine as soon as the yell galvanized their pilots into a run toward them.

Everyone's day started early. If the pilots were ready at dawn then the ground crews were up earlier, testing the engines, running them up and checking them over. Flight sergeants tried to get the most aircraft available following the previous day's battle damage. Each aircraft would have its daily inspection.

Most pilots were woken up still tired. Their cheery batmen would ignore the rude comments that would greet them as they woke their pilots. Once up those who could concentrate would gulp down mugs of tea before getting themselves down to the flights. They would look over their own aircraft, talk to the ground crew, ensure that their parachute was ready and that the flying helmet was in position, usually draped over the gun sight, ready to be pulled on as they sat in the cockpit and were strapped in by a crewman. Everyone hoped for bad weather but, generally speaking, the summer of 1940 was beautifully warm and sunny.

In the early days, many pilots were physically sick in the early mornings. In 74 Squadron for example, after they had washed, shaved and drunk a cup of tea, they would be off to the airfield. Before reaching dispersal, several of them were sick, usually getting rid of the last of the beer drunk the previous evening. Drinking the odd pint or two helped guarantee a few hours deep sleep – an important consideration. The squadron doctor wondered why this sickness occurred and discovered that being so early in the morning, coupled with nervous tension (this might be their last day

on earth), the body's sugar content was low, and breakfast was still some hours away. The problem was solved by having a handy supply of barley sugar sweets to suck.

There was no special flying clothing in 1940, pilots simply flew in something comfortable; an old uniform, with perhaps a jumper or pullover, covered perhaps by an overall. Neither the Hurricane or Spitfire had any cockpit heating and within minutes a pilot could be at 30,000 feet where the outside temperature was a good deal colder than on the ground! Irvin jackets too, although bulky, helped keep the body warm.

Sitting in the sun was pleasant enough but the ever-present danger was often just minutes away. At dawn readiness the pilots usually nodded off to sleep right away, they were half asleep anyway. If there had been a binge the night before, the pilot might trot over to his airplane and take a whiff of oxygen. Another method of sobering up was used by the medical officer. He would give the pilot a special mixture tasting oddly of toothpaste, which some pilots thought it was anyway. The pilots had to be prepared to give their all in the coming battle.

Death and destruction for the RAF and the Luftwaffe continued with the commencement of the third phase of the battle on 24 August. The shortage of RAF pilots had recently become critical. Support came from the Fleet Air Arm, who lent 56 pilots during the battle. A further 30 or so came from Bomber and Army Co-operation Commands. Some new squadrons also became available, a Polish, a Czech and a Canadian squadron helped to swell Fighter Command's ranks or fill a gap left by a unit pulled out of the front line for a rest.

On Saturday 24 August, airfields were attacked in the southeast of England. Manston was evacuated and Portsmouth was hit heavily. North Weald was bombed by 20 bombers which hit station buildings, two messes, the married quarters and stores, but otherwise did not affect the efficiency of the base.

By midafternoon Keith Park had all his squadrons airborne and engaged, so he requested help from Leigh-Mallory's 12 Group. Leigh-Mallory had been keen to try and form his squadrons into wings in order to bring a larger force of fighters into action at one time. This made sense but unfortunately it took time to organize once they were in the air and more often than not in the days ahead, the raiders were on their way home before the 12 Group Wing could get at them. On the 24th only the Spitfires of 19 Squadron became engaged after the failure of the wing to form over Duxford. The six pilots of 19 Squadron were flying cannon-armed Spitfires which were suffering from gun-stoppages at this stage of RAF cannon development. However, Flight Lieutenant B J E Lane's guns scored:

'I climbed up and at approximately 1610 hours got astern of a ragged formation of about 40 Me 110s and Do 215s, escorted by ten Me 109s above and to the rear. I approached from below . . . and almost got within range when 110s saw us and turned towards us. A dog-fight ensued and I opened fire from below and astern of nearest 110 but was forced to break away as tracer appeared over my head from enemy aircraft astern. Got below another 110 and fired slight deflection burst at port engine and observed a large part of engine or mainplane fly off. Enemy aircraft dived and I observed it crash into the sea.'

Another pilot, Sergeant R F Hamlyn of 610 Squadron claimed the destruction of five German aircraft during the day, in three hectic sorties. Altogether the RAF flew 936 sorties on the 24th, and lost 22 aircraft. The Luftwaffe losses totalled 38 during 1030 sorties.

The following day *Luftflotte* 3 sent a large force toward Weymouth. Nos 17, 87 and 609 Squadrons engaged this raid, destroying several raiders. Flying Officer Count M B Czernin of 17 Squadron shot down two and shared a third with 609 Squadron despite seeing his Commanding Officer shot down ahead of him during a battle with a gaggle of Me 110s:

'One broke. Chased and fired from above. Nose went down, EA burst into flames and crashed straight into the sea. Climbed and resumed attack. Beam attack and 110 broke away pouring smoke and went into a vertical dive, burst into flames and crashed into the sea. Resumed attack and had to break off a Spitfire on its tail firing at him. Shook him off and attacked 110

Above: A Heinkel He III perfectly aligned in a Hurricane's gun sight.
Right: Another member of 43 Squadron was John Simpson, seen here at Buckingham Palace on 6 August 1940 for investiture with a DFC.
Top left: Sergeant, later Wing Commander, R F 'Ronnie' Hamlyn, AFC, DFM of 610 Squadron, AAF.
Top center: Squadron leader B J E 'Sandy' Lane, DFC, commander of 19 Squadron at Duxford in 1940.
Top right: Flight Lieutenants Peter Townsend, DFC (left) and Caesar Hull, DFC of 43 'Fighting Cocks' Squadron. Hull, a South African, commanded the unit briefly before his death.

and after a long burst from quarter astern, nose dropped and it lost height . . . and glided down with both engines out. Broke off as obviously it was going to crash and saw two Spitfires attack it again. One baled out and then EA nose dived into a wood two miles SE of Dorchester and burst into flames.'

No 609 Squadron were in the thick of it and shot down four Me 110s and damaged several others. No 87 Squadron got three escorting Me 109s but lost one pilot, Sergeant S R E Wakeling. His voice came over the radio that he had had his hand blown off by a cannon shell but he thought he would make it to base. He did not. He probably fainted from loss of blood.

The pace was beginning to tell in many squadrons. No 32 Squadron, based at Biggin Hill, had sustained a number of casualties since mid-August and on the 18th lost five of its Hurricanes with four pilots wounded or with burns. It lost one more on the 22nd and on the 24th lost another five of its aircraft with one pilot wounded. On the 25th it lost two aircraft and one pilot. This reduced 32 Squadron's effective strength to eight. It was pulled out of the battle area.

In recent raids by the Luftwaffe, bombs had been dropped upon the suburbs of London. Although this was not planned by Luftwaffe leaders it led to a reprisal raid by Bomber Command on the night of 25/26 August, Berlin being the obvious target. Little damage was inflicted but the effect upon German morale was considerable. However, it started a chain of events which led to London being a major target for Luftwaffe bombers and swung the weight of their effort away from Dowding's reeling fighter bases.

However, that was still a few days off and in the meantime, RAF fighter airfields continued to be the primary target. No 1 Canadian Squadron moved from RAF Northolt to North Weald and saw its first major action in the afternoon of 26 August. No 616 Squadron, who had been involved in the raid against the northeast on 15

August and who had now moved south to Kenley, were hit badly. Scrambled to intercept raiders over Dungeness they arrived too late to engage the bombers but were attacked by a large force of Me 109s. Six of their aircraft were shot down, two pilots were killed and three others wounded. Meanwhile the Canadians were vectored onto a raid of Dornier 17s, escorted by Me 109s, but it was the bombers which inflicted the damage. Three Hurricanes were hit by accurate return fire from the German air gunners, killing one attacking pilot and forcing two other pilots to crash land, their aircraft were written off. One of the latter was the Commanding Officer, Squadron Leader E A McNab.

Portsmouth was attacked at around 1600 hours when 50 He 111s escorted by more than 100 single- and twin-engined Messerschmitts came in near the Isle of Wight. Between them 10 and 11 Groups sent up eight squadrons but only 43, 602 and 615 Squadrons managed to intercept. One pilot of 43 Squadron, Pilot Officer H L North, was wounded but:

'. . . I echeloned my section to port and attacked head-on a formation of six He 111s. They were the lower layer of a much larger mass stepped up. I could only fire the briefest of bursts and broke away below without noticing any results. I climbed back to the attack and got in two long . . . bursts. Quantities of smoke was emitted, the undercarriage dropped, one person at least baled out and the enemy was last seen diving, but I got hit by explosive shell which went into my shoulder and arm.'

Despite this wound, Pilot Officer North used up the remainder of his ammunition on another Heinkel which went down with one engine trailing smoke. Then North, having been hit again from behind, was forced to bale out.

It was not a good day for the Kenley squadrons, for in addition to 616 Squadron being bounced around midday, 615 Squadron lost four aircraft in the late afternoon, again by Me 109s. Keith Park's express

orders were for RAF pilots to avoid wasteful combats with German fighters and to get at the bombers but it was not always possible to totally ignore the deadly Messerschmitts.

In the final days of August, there was no let up by Luftwaffe aircraft in attacking airfields, indeed the action on 30 and 31 August was, according to some pilots, the bloodiest of the battle. In 1054 sorties and 978 sorties respectively, the RAF lost 25 fighters on the 30th with 10 pilots killed, and 39 on the 31st with 14 pilots lost – some of the heaviest casualties of the battle. On the same dates the Germans lost 36 and 41 respectively.

Detling was bombed on the 30th and so was Biggin Hill, which reduced the base to a shambles and left 39 dead and 26 injured. One of the casualties on the 31st was the Commanding Officer of 253 Squadron, Squadron Leader T P Gleave. Gleave had shot down four Me 109s on the previous day.

Having led seven Hurricanes off, which was all that was left of Gleave's unit, they engaged enemy bombers. Returning to his base at Kenley, Gleave was hit from behind and below by an Me 109, which set his Hurricane on fire. The first thing he knew of the enemy's presence was a shattering crash as the whole of the instrument panel disappeared in front of his eyes. Bullets hit the reserve gasoline tank located between the panel and the engine, setting it on fire and spraying 28 gallons of gasoline in his lap. Fortunately Gleave had his cockpit canopy locked open so he was able to quickly release his harness and push forward on the stick. As the burning Hurricane went over the vertical he was shot straight out. His clothes were on fire so he chose not to open his parachute for fear of it too catching fire. He fell a couple of thousand feet, felt cooler so pulled the ripcord. As luck would have it he had broken his goggles the day before and had not had time to replace them. Consequently, when his face was badly burned, his eyelids were stuck closed together. Yet he could clearly hear the unmistakable sound of a Messerschmitt's engine as it came near but luckily it was forced away by a Spitfire. With that danger passed he managed to prise his eyes open and shortly afterward hit the ground in a clearing in the middle of a wood. He was terribly burned. Apart from his face and eyelids, his trousers had been burned away and skin on both legs had lifted and draped his legs like outsize plus fours. His gloves had been almost burned off and the skin from his wrists and hands hung down like paper bags. The underside of his right arm and elbow were also burned. As he sat in the clearing he came to the conclusion that the services of a doctor might be necessary!

Another commander wounded on the 31st was Squadron Leader P W Townsend of 85 Squadron operating from Croydon. Bombs began to fall on the east side of the airfield as the Hurricanes became airborne.

They, like 253 Squadron, had been sent off too late. Climbing at full throttle and with black mushrooms of exploding antiaircraft shells staining the sky to the south above Biggin Hill, they could see Me 110s above. As the fight began, Townsend pushed his cockpit hood back so as to see the enemy better. Then Me 109s came diving down. Townsend fought one, sending it down belching smoke. Engaging another he could see an Me 110 heading toward him, its guns flashing. His Hurricane took hits and his left foot was knocked off the rudder pedals as gasoline gushed into the cockpit. His machine dived, trailing smoke but luckily it did not catch fire. In front of him his windshield was starred with bullet marks for the bulletproof screen had taken the enemy's slugs. Moments later he took to his parachute with a wounded foot.

At RAF Hornchurch that same day, raiders screamed in and caught 54 Squadron on the ground as they struggled to get airborne. An estimated 60 bombs hit along a line from the dispersal pens to the gasoline dump and beyond. The last three Spitfires were caught and all were totally wrecked, but all three pilots miraculously survived. Flight Lieutenant A C Deere had one wing and his propeller blown off, the machine turned over and plowed along the airfield on its back. Sergeant J Davis was blown across two fields and into a river while Pilot Officer E F Edsall was blown up but landed right side up. He scrambled clear to help Deere out of his smashed airplane as bombs continued to rain down. All three pilots were ready for action the next day.

As August ended it became evident to Luftwaffe commanders that despite the claims of its fighter pilots, the RAF was far from being knocked out of the sky. They also realized that the output of fighter production from British factories and from repair depots, had been considerably underestimated. The German bomber crews continued to report aggressive actions by RAF fighters. There was not the slightest sign that the British boys were relaxing in their determination to get to grips with the enemy.

Despite this view, Fighter Command's reserves were running dangerously low but it could just maintain support for 10, 11 and 12 Group's losses. Dowding's main concern was for pilots, especially leaders. A dozen squadron commanders had been killed or wounded and nearly 40 flight commanders had similarly been knocked out. On some sorties, sections, flights and, on occasion, even whole squadrons were led by junior officers and experienced non-commissioned officer pilots, such as Ginger Lacey (501 Squadron), Geoffrey Allard (85), Archie McDowell (602) and 'Grumpy' Unwin (19). Of all the experienced fighter pilots in Dowding's force, there were only about 500 officers or sergeants and each had to fly four, five or even six sorties each day.

It was inevitable that replacement pilots from training units had not the length of

Above center: Alan Deere (left) and Colin Gray, two New Zealanders who fought with 54 Squadron during the battle.
Above right: Flight Lieutenant Geoffrey 'Sammy' Allard, DFC, DFM of 85 Squadron. An ex-Halton aircraft apprentice, Allard fought in France and the battle over Britain, claiming two dozen victories; only to die in a simple flying accident in 1941.
Above left: J H 'Ginger' Lacey, DFM, one of the leading scorers during the battle, who flew with 501 Squadron, AAF.
Above: Pilots found the Spitfire highly maneuverable and easy to fly.
Left: Group of 19 Squadron Spitfire pilots at Duxford, 1940. Seated on the wing are Squadron Leader B J E Lane, DFC (OC) and Flight Sergeant 'Grumpy' Unwin, DFM.

training that would have been desirable. Some became easy prey to a still victorious Luftwaffe fighter arm. The squadrons were taking a battering. No 151 Squadron was pulled back from the front, down to 10 aircraft and 12 pilots. No 56, without a Commanding Officer and with only seven aircraft went to a quieter location. No 43 had lost two Commanding Officers and its third, Squadron Leader C B Hull, was to last just one week. No 610 Squadron was about to leave for the north and a rest. The fate of Britain now rested totally on the young shoulders of Fighter Command's fighter pilots as September began.

The first day of September saw the continuance of attacks on air bases with four major assaults. Biggin Hill was attacked for the sixth time in three days. No 79 Squadron was now Biggin's only defense and pilots returning from an interception found the airfield pitted with bomb craters, forcing them to divert to Croydon. Eastchurch, Detling and the docks at Tilbury were other targets. Over 120 raiders returned to these targets after lunch while two further raids went for Hawkinge, Lymne and Detling in the late afternoon. In the last raid Biggin was hit yet again, knocking out the operations room. Four Spitfires were also destroyed and the armory set ablaze.

On 2 September, there were four raids. This time Eastchurch, North Weald, Rochford and again Biggin Hill were attacked. The raiders totalled around 250 aircraft, an awe-inspiring sight for individual squadrons to see flying in.

Two tragic losses occurred on the 1st and 2nd. Two fighter-pilot brothers fell within hours of each other. On 1 September Flying Officer Patrick Woods-Scawen of 85 Squadron died when leading his section.

No 85 Squadron was led by Flight Sergeant Allard against a vast armada of aircraft, but enemy fighters hurled themselves at the squadron to shoot down five of the Hurricanes. One pilot was killed, two wounded and one missing (the fifth crash landed unhurt). The missing pilot was Woods-Scawen who was found on the 6th – his parachute had failed to open. The next day his brother Tony, flying with 43 Squadron, was shot down by Me 109s just 24 hours after his brother. Both had won the DFC in the battle.

Also on the 2nd, Pilot Officer R H Hillary of 603 Squadron shot down two Me 109s, probably a third and damaged a fourth in three sorties. On the second sortie, just after midday:

'When five miles off Sheppey I saw a formation of 109s. I chased one over to France and fired at it. I saw the EA's perspex hood break up but as it was a head-on attack I was unable to see anything more of it. I then saw a squadron of 109s at the same height as myself, 23,000 feet . . . I attacked outside Me 109 with three short bursts and saw it spin down emitting black and white smoke. After a few seconds it caught fire.'

Sergeant J H Ginger Lacey, flying in 501 Squadron, also destroyed an Me 109. He saw three Messerschmitts about to dive on his squadron and climbed to engage them:

'I was able to get in a good burst of about five seconds at a red cowled Me 109, but the EA immediately turned and I was unable to bring my guns to bear, but after about 30 seconds of circling, the Me 109 pilot jumped out and did a delayed drop of about 5,000 feet before opening his parachute.'

The next day, the first anniversary of the war, more heavy attacks were directed against the southern airfields, the now familiar build up of aircraft over Calais coming onto the radar screens around 0800 hours. Their allotted targets were Hornchurch, North Weald and Debden, although North Weald was the only one reached by the raiders. One of the defending fighter pilots was the same Richard Hillary of 603 Squadron who had done so well the day before. He later wrote of his feelings as he sat in his Spitfire following the scramble call:

'I felt the usual sick feeling in the pit of my stomach, as though I was about to run a race, and then I was too busy getting into position to feel anything.'

Below: 'Red' Tobin, 'Shorty' Keough, and 'Andy' Mamedoff; three US pilots who fought in the Battle of Britain.

Above: A Heinkel He III has its starboard engine shattered by a Spitfire's guns.

Above right: Trio from 242 Squadron at Coltishall. Flight Lieutenant W L 'Willie' McKnight, DFC, Squadron Leader Douglas Bader, DSO, and Flight Lieutenant Eric Ball, DFC. McKnight and Ball were later killed on operations.
Below: Hurricanes of 242 Squadron.

Making the mistake of following a 109 for too long he was himself attacked from behind. His Spitfire burst into flames and for several agonizing seconds he was trapped in the blazing cockpit before the machine broke up and he was flung into space. He, like Tom Gleave, was very badly burned and spent months in hospital. Later he wrote his classic book *The Last Enemy*.

Sergeant D Fopp of 17 Squadron was also shot down and burned on the 3rd:

'We were scrambled late and did not get sufficient altitude to achieve a favourable attacking position from above, with the result that we had to attack head-on at about 20,000 feet, and hope to break up the large formation of Do 17s, with guns blazing which did separate them considerably. I had just put a Dornier's engine out and he was smoking badly when I saw three Me 110s coming in behind in line astern. By this time I had run out of ammunition but decided that as I could not match them for speed I would turn into them and simulate an attack. This I did and to my astonishment and joy they broke all round me so I immediately half rolled and dived for the deck. Unfortunately for me one of them was also below and behind out of sight and managed to put a cannon shell into my radiator, with the result that all I heard was a thump and the next second I was sitting in a ball of fire.'

Fopp managed to bale out and put out his smoldering tunic and trousers. He landed in trees but got out of his harness safely, walked out of the wood and met two farm laborers. In his condition he could have been any nationality but his language was such that they were quickly convinced that he was British!

Pilot Officer D W Hanson, also of 17 Squadron, shot down a Dornier in this action but his machine was hit by return fire. Hanson had difficulty in getting out of his Hurricane and when finally he suc-ceeded he was only 100 feet up. His parachute failed to deploy in the short drop and he was killed when he hit the ground, almost at the same moment as his machine crashed on Foulness Island.

Honors were even on the war's first anniversary – 16 Germans shot down, for 16 RAF fighters and eight pilots.

It was slightly better the next day, 25 Germans for 17 RAF machines. The Germans went for sector RAF stations and the Vickers factory at Brooklands. A force of Me 110s got through the defenses by flying at low level and following the railroad track over Guildford. They hit Brooklands, where Wellington bombers were being built. Alert ground gunners shot down two Me 100s and others hurriedly got rid of their bombs, as Hurricanes of 253 Squadron got in among them, but nevertheless the Germans did considerable damage. Some 88 workers were killed and 600 were injured. Output almost stopped for four days as machine and erecting shops were badly damaged.

Several Me 110s were shot down by the Hurricanes.

No 253 Squadron was based at Kenley, sharing the base with 66 Squadron who did not have a good day. They lost five of their Spitfires and all the pilots involved were wounded. No 222 Squadron from Hornchurch lost three Spitfires and two pilots were killed. As if enemy fighters were not dangerous enough, Pilot Officer J M V Carpenter was hit by 'friendly' anti-aircraft fire over Kent and blown out of his cockpit. He landed in his parachute with only slight injuries.

The next day 66 Squadron lost three more aircraft, while 41 Squadron lost five including the squadron commander and one flight commander. No 19 Squadron also lost its commanding officer on the 5th.

On Friday 6 September, the final day of phase three, it was the Polish pilots of 303 Squadron who suffered at the hands of the Luftwaffe. Five of their aircraft were shot down although no pilots were killed. The Squadron's joint Commanding Officers, Squadron Leader R G Kellet, an Englishman, and Squadron Leader Z Krasno-

debski, were both wounded. Both British flight commanders were also shot down and a Polish noncommissioned officer was wounded.

Four pilots from 601 Squadron based at Tangmere were shot down, two of whom were killed. One was Flying Officer C R Davis, an experienced South African pilot with several victories to his name, the other was Flying Officer Willie Rhodes-Moorhouse.

The Luftwaffe lost 378 of its aircraft during the third phase. The margin between victory and defeat was now very slender.

Below: Messerschmitt Bf 109E-4 of II/JG3 piloted by Oberleutnant Franz von Werra, shot down by 234 Squadron Spitfire over Kent in the afternoon of 5 September 1940.

Bottom: In theory the Spitfire was supposed to tackle the high-flying Messerschmitt cover formations and leave the bomber formations to the slower Hurricane.
Below: The erks (airmen) of 602 Squadron, AAF refuel and rearm a unit Spitfire.

4.THE BLITZ

The battle's fourth phase, marked by a change of tactics by the Luftwaffe, began on 7 September. It was clear now to the Luftwaffe High Command that RAF resistance was far from decreasing. During the period 24 August to 6 September, over 100 bombers had been lost despite the orders to German fighter pilots to stick close and defend the bomber formations. It appeared also that despite continual raids on RAF airfields, they were not being knocked out for any appreciable length of time.

Some believed that London should be the direct target, thereby causing the civilian population to crack and force the British Government to capitulate. Bombs had in fact been dropped on London by navigational error on the night of 25 August, which caused the reprisal raid already mentioned. Hitler gave Goering a free hand and it was just as well for Britain that he did, for Goering ended his attacks on RAF airfields in order to concentrate on the plum of a prize – London. It was to prove an incalculable error, but it saved Fighter Command. Plans were immediately put into operation to fly against London and the first assault took place on the 7th.

Prepared for further attacks on its airfields, the RAF were not even considering a raid on London when the radar screens showed a massive armada of aircraft heading toward the Thames Estuary – 300

Above: The aftermath of a raid on Coventry.
Left: London Docks after the first mass raid on London, 7 September 1940.

Right: The sky over Westminster recalls Stephen Spender's lines, '. . . and left the vivid air signed with their honour.'

bombers escorted by 600 fighters in two waves. The first wave flew direct to the Estuary, the other passed over Central London before turning back to the Estuary and the East End of London. Caught on the hop, the defending RAF fighters were unable to engage before many of the German aircraft had dropped their bombs. So while the airfields were being adequately defended, the road to London was open. Finally 11 Group got some units to intercept the huge armada and thereafter Hurricanes and Spitfires tried to nibble at them all the way back to the coast. It was to cost both sides dearly.

No 12 Group's Big Wing got into action, with 19, 242 and 310 Squadrons making preparations, when antiaircraft fire attracted them to part of the raid near North Weald. Squadron Leader B J E Lane, now Commanding Officer of 19 Squadron, saw them and attacked:

'A 110 dived in front of me and I led A Flight after it. Two Hurricanes were also attacking it. I fired a short burst as well as the other aircraft. Two baled out, one parachute failing to open. Enemy aircraft crashed one mile east of Hornchurch and one crewman landed nearby and was taken

prisoner of war.'

Flight Lieutenant J H G McArthur of 609 Squadron went for a formation of bombers which he took to be Dorniers. (Dornier 17s and Me 110s were often confused during the battle):

'I went for the nearest bomber and opened fire at about 400 yards, meanwhile experiencing very heavy return crossfire from the bomber formation. After about 12 seconds smoke started to come from the port motor and it left the formation. . . . I waited until it got down to about 3000 feet and then dived vertically on to it and fired off the rest of my ammunition. It kept going on down seemingly still under some sort of control, until it hit the water about 10 miles out from the centre of the Thames Estuary.'

Casualties among the RAF defenders totalled 28 fighters and 19 pilots. Some were experienced pilots and leaders. No 43 Squadron lost Ceasar Hull, who had won his DFC in the Norwegian campaign earlier in the year, and Flight Lieutenant R C Reynell, the Hawker test pilot who was flying operationally with the squadron. No

Above: Hurricane in markings of 111 Squadron.
Top right: The freak effect of a bomb blast on the night of 8/9 September 1940. Luckily the crew was in a nearby shelter.
Right: Dorniers from KG3 over Canning Town, London, on 7 September 1940.
Left: Air-to-air view of a Dornier bomber formation.

234 Squadron lost its Commanding Officer, Joe O'Brien, as well as its senior Flight Commander, Flight Lieutenant P C Hughes, DFC, who had claimed 16 victories in two months. Hughes was attacking a Dornier when its wing ripped off and smashed into his Spitfire, causing him to crash. No 257 Squadron was bounced by Me 109s and lost four aircraft and two pilots, including Flight Lieutenant H R A Beresford. It was not until 1979 that his remains and his shattered Hurricane were found in marshy ground on the Isle of Sheppey. No 303 Polish Squadron lost two aircraft with two more damaged. One of the damaged aircraft was flown by the British Flight Lieutenant A S Forbes who was slightly wounded. No 249 Squadron from North Weald lost six Hurricanes and one pilot plus three more wounded in fights with Me 109s.

German casualties totalled 41, of which 15 were Me 109s and seven were 110s. London had been heavily bombed and nearly 450 people had been killed in both central and suburban areas with over 1300 injured. The new phase in the Luftwaffe's offensive against Britain had begun. London and its populace would now have to 'take it' but at least the pressure was taken off Dowding's sorely pressed fighter bases. In addition the Luftwaffe began flying against London by night.

The next day the air action was light by recent comparisons and only night raids affected London, but on the 9th the battle flared again. London was bombed and

raids were directed against factories in the Thames Estuary area as well as Brooklands. Some 28 German aircraft were shot down as against 19 British machines. Two days later, on 11 September, the losses were 25 German aircraft and a depressing 29 RAF aircraft with 17 pilots killed and six others wounded, during raids on London, Portsmouth and Southampton.

Keith Park was now, whenever possible, ordering paired squadrons to be used together. When squadrons at 'readiness' were sent against early raiders, the Spitfires would take on the escort fighters while an accompanying Hurricane unit went for the bombers. In their turn, the 'available' – 15 minutes – squadrons, brought to the 'readiness' state also in like pairs, to be ready to deal with subsequent waves of raiders. The 'available' – at 30 minutes – squadrons were then used singly to reinforce those units already engaged or to protect specific factory or airfield targets.

On the 11th, big enemy formations began to build up over Calais and Ostend in the early afternoon while others began to fly in from the Seine area and Cherbourg. Shortly afterward waves of Me 109s were in evidence over Kent. It was these Me 109s, as well as close escort 109s, that caused many of the RAF casualties.

Only two RAF pilots were lost on 12 September, but one was Wing Commander J S Dewar DSO, DFC, Wing Commander at Exeter and late Commanding Officer of 87 Squadron. He had been visiting friends at Tangmere and took off with them during

Above: Hurricanes of 303 *Kosciuszko* Squadron, Northolt in late September 1940.
Top right: Members of 303 (Polish) Squadron at Northolt, September 1940. From left: Z Henneberg, J A Kent (a Canadian Flight Commander) and M Feric.
Below: Hurricane pilots of 1 Squadron, RCAF at Northolt on 12 September 1940.

Right: Czech pilots of 310 Squadron at Duxford on 1 September 1940. Formed on 10 July, the unit flew its first combat sorties on 26 August. Kneeling, in RAF uniform, is Flight Lieutenant A Jefferies, DFC, an English Flight Commander.
Below: Surviving crew members of a Heinkel He III being escorted from their crash at Burmash, Kent on 11 September — victims of a Spitfire pilot.

A view of a Hurricane coded in 242 Squadron markings.

48

Below: Heinkel He III crew survey bullet damage to their crashed bomber in France on return from a sortie.

Bottom: Hurricane RF-E, P3700, of 303 *Kosciuszko* Squadron at Northolt in September 1940.

Right: The remains of Hauptmann
Ernst Püttman's KG3 Dornier Do 17Z-2
in the forecourt of Victoria Station,
London on 15 September 1940.
Below right: Antiaircraft guns fire at
the enemy in London.
Below: Sergeant Josef Frantisek, a
Czech fighter who served with 303
(Polish) Squadron, scoring at least
16 victories. He was fated to die in a
landing accident on 8 October 1940.

an alert. He failed to return and later his
bullet-ridden body was found where he
had fallen in his parachute. A few days
later one of his old 87 Squadron's pilots
chased a bomber 20 miles out to sea to shoot
it down in personal revenge for Dewar's
death.

The issue of shooting up pilots in their
parachutes is a controversial one, but it did
happen from time to time on both sides.
One former Battle of Britain pilot told this
author that in his squadron they had an
unwritten law that if a German pilot was in
his parachute over the French coast or
within 10 miles of it they might have a go
at him, but not if he was coming down over
England or off the English coast. One of his
companions was always for shooting them
up wherever he found them!

The 13 September was also quiet, although one of the RAF's successful non-
commissioned officer pilots, Ginger Lacey,
had to take to his parachute after engaging
an He 111 over Kent. It was a cloudy day
and Lacey had volunteered to go up to try
to locate a reported raider. Guided by
ground control he found his prey and shot
it down but his Hurricane was hit by
return fire and he had to bale out. Later he
was told that this Heinkel had bombed
Buckingham Palace.

London was again attacked on the 14th
although poor weather prevented any large-
scale assault until the afternoon. A little
after 1500 hours three raiders crossed the
English coast and headed in along two
routes – the Estuary and over Kent. Most
of the raiders were fighters and in the
scraps which occurred honors proved even,
14 to each side.

Yet it was to be the next day which
turned out to be significant in many
respects. For ever afterward, 15 September
every year has been set aside as the Anniversary Day of the Battle of Britain. It saw
the Germans heavily defeated in the air and
ultimately the Germans were forced to
change their policy against Britain.

For the Germans it was a repeat of the
7 September raid, in that it was supposed
to be a prelude to invasion. Hitler had
postponed his planned assault by sea and
air, from early September to the 11th.
Then he postponed it again to the 17th.
However, the disastrous results of the
15th caused him to postpone the invasion
indefinitely. While it is felt in some quarters
that Hitler never seriously considered invading Britain, there is no doubt whatsoever
that the people of Britain, and especially
the war leaders, could see no other course
open to Hitler.

By 1100 hours on Sunday 15 September
mass formations of German aircraft clearly
showed on the radar screens. Even at this
stage the Germans had not totally realized
how accurately the radar plots could identify
size, course and height of their raids. No
11 Group scrambled 11 squadrons, 10
Group one and 12 Group its Big Wing of
five squadrons.

As the Germans flew in from the coast
toward London, in layers from 15,000–
26,000 feet, they were continually harassed
by RAF fighters whose young pilots flung
themselves relentlessly at the vast horde of
black-crossed bombers and fighters.

The tenacity of the RAF fighter pilots
as well as the sheer number of fighters they
could see, must have come as a great shock
to many Luftwaffe flyers. It had been
confidently predicted that Fighter Command was down to its last 'handful' of
aircraft, and yet the Luftwaffe could see

flight after flight, squadron after squadron, heading straight for them, their wing guns blazing. One of the attackers was Flying Officer J C Dundas of 609:

'(We) turned towards enemy aircraft which we identified as Dorniers and turned to intercept. There were many 109s on both sides of the bombers and above them. . . . I turned and attacked the EA in centre of formation from below and from the beam. As I passed I saw one of its motors stop. On breaking away I was attacked by a 109 from above and astern. . . . I was chased off by three 109s which peeled off from 20,000 feet above, but who gave themselves away by opening fire from excessive range.'

Squadron Leader J Sample, Commanding Officer of 504 Squadron also got in among the Dorniers. He attacked one which broke formation streaming smoke. Looking down he clearly saw the famous bend in the River Thames and also picked out the Oval cricket ground:

'I found myself below another Dornier which had white smoke coming from it. It was being attacked by two Hurricanes and a Spitfire. . . . I went to join in. I climbed up above and did a diving attack on him. Coming in to attack I noticed what appeared to be a red light shining in the rear gunner's cockpit but when I got closer I realised I was looking right through the gunner's cockpit into the pilot and observer's cockpit beyond. The red light was fire. I gave it a quick burst and as I passed him on the right I looked through

the big glass nose of the Dornier. It was like a furnace inside. He began to go down and we watched. In a few seconds the tail came off and the bomber did a forward somersault and then went into a spin. After he had done two turns in his spin his wings broke off outboard of the engines.'

Sergeant R T Holmes of Sample's Squadron gained undying fame by shooting down a Dornier which crashed into the forecourt of Victoria Station. Holmes was hit by return fire and baled out, only to land ingloriously in a Chelsea garbage can.

As the assault continued into the afternoon, other units took to the air. One pilot airborne was the Station Commander of RAF Northolt, a fighter pilot from World War I, Group Captain S F Vincent. He was near Biggin Hill when he saw 18 Dorniers escorted by 20 Me 109s above:

'There was no other British fighters in sight, so I made a head-on attack on the first section of the bombers, opening fire at 600 yards and closing to 200 yards. I saw my DeWilde ammunition hit the EA. On breaking away I noticed that five of the bombers had turned round and were proceeding due south. I made further attacks on the retreating bombers . . . and could see the DeWilde hitting in each attack. One Dornier left the formation and lost height. With no ammunition left I could not finish it off.'

John Dundas was back in the air for another crack and again found Dornier bombers, this time above Rye:

'Red section attacked the rear wing of Dorniers and as they did so two Dorniers detached themselves from formation and tried to dive away. I selected one and went in after it had been attacked by a number of Red Section. Fired from 300 to 150 yards and closed to dead astern and slightly above. At first I experienced return fire and was twice hit. Then pieces began to fall off and flames came from its starboard wing and engine. After breaking away I saw EA spin down and members of the crew escape by parachute.'

Pilot Officer P S Turner, flying with 242 Squadron in 12 Group's Wing, was in the action, sending down an Me 109 probably destroyed before he attacked a Dornier from KG2:

'. . . observed a Do 215, attacked from abeam using full deflection. His starboard engine started to smoke, the 215 then slid into a gentle dive. It hit the ground and exploded between some houses on the north bank of the Thames east of Hornchurch. No people left the aircraft.'

Yet again German Intelligence estimates were wrong. The RAF's 'last 50 Spitfires' was only a figure on their reports. Although at the time an inflated figure of 185 German aircraft shot down put great heart into the British people and the RAF pilots, the true figure was 60. Even so, with damaged machines taken into account it was a savage blow to the Luftwaffe, particularly in view of recent air losses. The RAF lost 26 fighters.

Below: Messerschmitt Bf 109E of II/JG3 *Udet* after its ultimate sortie over England.

5. THE TURNING POINT

Bottom: WAAFs plot the progress of the battle.
Below: Adolf Galland (center) and Werner Mölders talking with Ernst Udet, Chief of the Luftwaffe's Technical Branches, during a visit to the 'Channel Front' by Udet on 4 September 1940.

Although the battle was to rage for several more weeks and the RAF fighter pilots had to continue their constant air actions against the Luftwaffe, it has now become accepted that 15 September was the turning point. As if to accentuate the victory of the 15th, the skies over southern England stayed comparatively quiet on the 16th.

Goering called a conference with his air commanders. Although presumably shaken by the losses of the previous day he showed little sign of it and merely informed his commanders that there was to be a return to a policy of knocking out the RAF – a task he felt would now only take four or five days. In this he was supported by his Intelligence people who still continued to underestimate both the RAF's front-line strength and reserves. These reserves now numbered 160 with a further 400 available for delivery in seven days.

Goering also decided to reduce the bomber formations but to support them with maximum fighter cover in order to blast the British fighters as they came up to engage the raids. London would continue to be raided by night.

The 11 Group commander, Keith Park, was also adjusting his tactics. He felt that his squadrons could do better if more were able to engage the enemy. Specifically, he wanted the Spitfires from Biggin Hill and Hornchurch to engage the Me 109s, while Hurricanes, operating in groups of three if time allowed them to get together, from Northolt and Tangmere, went for the bombers. It also became clear that the claim of 185 kills on the 15th was not supported by crashed aircraft on the ground, and the figure was being revised.

Activity was still reduced on the 18th although it was obvious to the RAF that a large fighter sweep flown by the Luftwaffe in the afternoon was designed solely in order to produce a fighter-versus-fighter action. In an attempt to carry out Goering's directives, the Luftwaffe mounted another sweep the following morning, followed by a small raiding force of Ju 88s escorted by 100 Messerschmitts. This was ignored by the RAF as its intention was too obvious. Therefore, another force of Ju 88s was sent in. This was met by a large force of Hurricanes and Spitfires, including the 12 Group Duxford Wing. Nine Ju 88s were quickly destroyed by 92 Squadron and the Big Wing, although the Wing claimed 30 victories!

The most significant event on the 19th was that Hitler finally shelved his plans to invade England and ordered the prepared invasion fleet of barges and troops to be dispersed. This latter fact was confirmed by RAF reconnaissance who, naturally, had been taking a keen interest in watching this force grow in recent weeks in the Channel ports along the French coast.

Over the next few days Luftwaffe activity was slight, confined mostly to fighter sweeps. Then on the 27th the fury returned. At 0800 hours activity was recorded on Operations Tables – bomb-carrying Me 109s and Me 110s headed in toward London on a broad front from Dover to Brighton. The 11 Group fighters harried

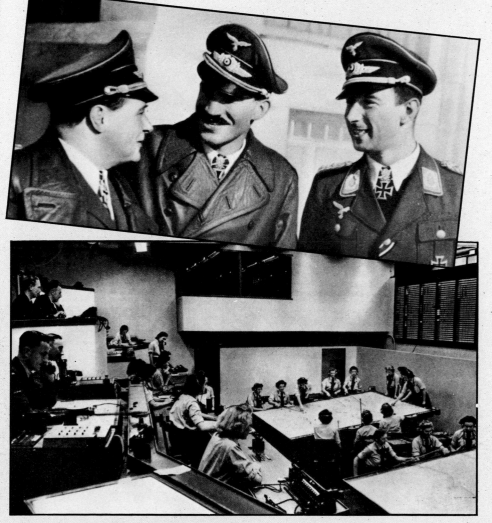

them all the way to the outskirts of London. The Germans remained over the southeast, trying to exhaust the defender's fuel and ammunition supplies preparatory to a raid by Ju 88s. However, the bombers failed to pick up their heavy escort and met over 100 defending fighters who promptly set about the raiders. Urgent calls for supporting Me 109s brought in a large force of Messerschmitts and both raiders and defenders suffered losses. Twelve Ju 88s went crashing earthward in this battle. One of the defending Me 109s was shot down by Pilot Officer R G A Barclay of 249 Squadron:

'I chased a 109 which dived very steeply. I had to use automatic boost cut-out to catch up the 109. I lost the 109 in haze owing to its camouflage against the ground, but it suddenly climbed almost vertically out of the haze. I closed to about 150 yards and fired about four bursts, one almost vertically up at the 109, one almost vertically down at the 109, two bursts from the beam. The EA poured glycol. The cockpit roof flew off. The pilot baled out successfully. The EA crashed on a farm SW of Ashford.'

Later, on the Squadron's third sortie of the day, Barclay destroyed a Ju 88 but had to force land at West Malling when his Hurricane was hit by an Me 109's snap burst. Pilot Officer A G Lewis of 249 claimed six victories on this day, three Me 109s, two Me 110s and a Ju 88. He also damaged another Me 109 and probably destroyed a Me 110. It brought his personal score to 18.

Further west 80 aircraft were heading for Bristol; He 111s and bomb-carrying Me 110s escorted by more Me 110s, came over the coast. This raid was met by five RAF squadrons. The Heinkels were split up and sent scurrying for the coast, the Me 110s pressed on to Bristol but were hotly engaged by RAF fighters. One escorting Me 110 was shot down by Pilot Officer M C Maxwell of 56 Squadron who wrongly identified it as a Dornier. Having scrambled with his squadron, Maxwell had to land again, but taking off shortly afterward he engaged the returning force on his own:

'At 16,000 feet saw a formation of about 25 EA ahead at 18,000 feet, climbed and made a stern attack on rear aircraft. I then broke away and saw EA losing height with black smoke emitting from port engine. Another Hurricane attacked EA which dived steeply and later I attacked again after Hurricane broke away, and saw EA with one engine stopped, crash after endeavouring to force-land.'

Total losses by the Luftwaffe numbered 55 including 21 bombers; the RAF lost 28 fighters. At the time the day ranked with 15 August and 15 September as a victory against the German Air Force.

In contrast the 28th saw a victory for the

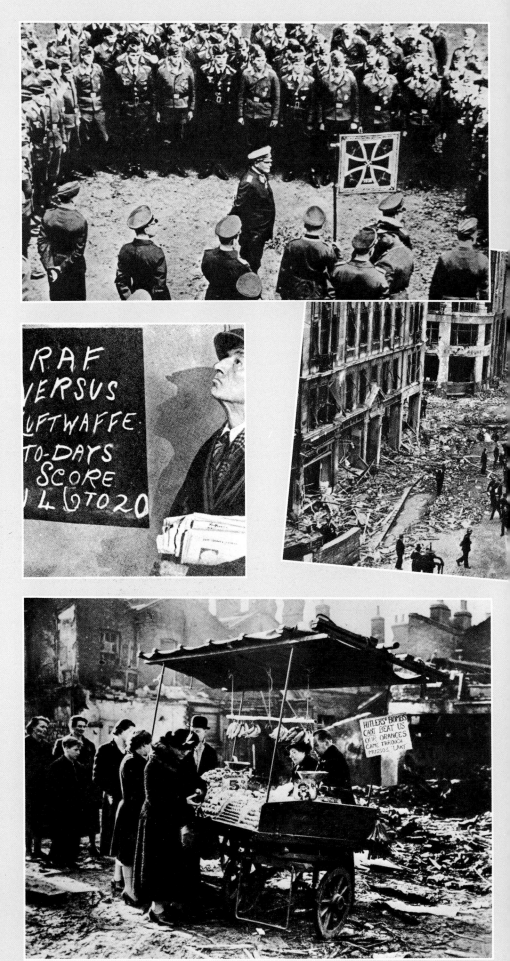

Left: Hermann Goering addresses his air crews.
Below left: British newspapers gave the score for each day.
Bottom left: Cockney humor and the carry-on spirit during the Blitz.

Above: St Clement Danes church, the RAF's church, after a bombing raid.
Left: Havoc in a London street which became a familiar sight to commuters.
Below: A mobile YMCA canteen at an antiaircraft-gun site.

Luftwaffe fighters, for during attacks on London and the Solent they shot down 16 RAF aircraft and only lost two of their own in actual combat. One of the RAF men shot down was A G Lewis who had scored so heavily the previous day. Me 109s hit him over Faversham – he baled out with burns.

The final fury of September came on the final day of the month when Me 109s flew sweeps toward London in the morning. No 229 Squadron suffered badly, losing four Hurricanes and four damaged in fights with Me 109s, with one pilot killed and three others wounded. This raid was followed by Me 109s and Me 110s attacking the Weymouth area and then after lunch Ju 88s and Me 109s again made for London. The final raid consisted of He 111s and Me 110s going for the Westland factory at Yeovil. No 56 Squadron was attacked by Me 110s, losing five Hurricanes with two others damaged, but luckily no pilots were lost. No 152 Squadron also tangled with the Me 110s, losing one pilot and aircraft and damaging four Spitfires. However, overall the Germans lost 47 aircraft during the day, to the RAF's 20. Most of the Luftwaffe's casualties were Me 109s.

We now realize that by the end of September the battle had effectively been won in the air. The German Luftwaffe could no longer sustain the losses which Fighter Command had inflicted upon it and tactics were again changed. The battle was continued by the Germans but now fighters generally flew alone, many carrying bombs. It became known as 'Messerschmitt Month.'

6. CLEARING THE SKIES

The October battles were in many ways more dangerous than the hectic days of the previous weeks. The Me 109s flew high, often above 25,000 feet, and the RAF fighters had to climb hard through hazy autumn sunshine and cloud to reach them. The advantage was usually held by the Me 109s above. During these weeks the RAF lost many veteran fighters in this moment of victory.

For the defenders it was impossible to know which of the Messerschmitts carried bombs and which did not. Also, once those carrying bombs had dropped them they became again a dangerous adversary.

One veteran pilot shot down and wounded on the very first day of October was Pilot Officer G H Bennions of 41 Squadron. Having already shot down 11 German aircraft plus five probables, he was due for leave but wanted to bring his score to a neat dozen. Flying high on patrol he became separated from his companions when he went after a bunch of Me 109s, one of which he destroyed. His machine was then hit and a cannon shell exploded by the left side of his face. His left eye was destroyed and a hole in his skull exposed his brain. In addition he sustained wounds to his right arm and leg. He managed to bale out and it was pure willpower that ultimately pulled him through.

Skirmishes occurred during the first week of October in poor weather. This improved on Monday the 7th, and the Luftwaffe sent an almost continuous stream of Me 109s over southeast England and later a Ju 88 raid was made against the Westland plant at Yeovil. Among the RAF scorers was the 'boss' of 609 Squadron, who had taken command of the squadron two days previously, Squadron Leader M L Robinson:

'It was extremely bright and as we were heading into the sun it was very difficult to pick out the EA which were now ahead of. . . . saw a circle of 110s directly ahead of us and proceeded to attack. I broke away downwards without seeing the result of the attack and I climbed up and attacked a separate 110 from astern. A Hurricane carried out a deflection shot between 110 and myself but I went on firing when the Hurricane broke away and the 110 dived vertically down with its port motor smoking.'

Minutes later he shot down a second 110 which dived into the ground north of the coastline. The day ended with 21 German and 17 RAF aircraft lost.

The RAF was now flying patrol lines in order to be in the air and ready to engage hostile raids. When the raids came in, other squadrons took off to be covered by those already airborne. Once the new squadron was at a good height, then the covering squadron could be sent to engage raiders or land to refuel as necessary. However, with Me 109s flying as high as 32,000 feet, it was a dangerous game, the Me 109s always holding the advantage of height. It took the average Spitfire Mk 1 18 minutes to climb to 25,000 feet, and 21 minutes for a Hurricane.

On 8 October the RAF lost only four aircraft but managed to shoot down 14 Germans. One of the Allied pilots lost was Sergeant Joseph Frantisek, a Czech pilot flying with 303 Polish Squadron. He had already destroyed 17 Luftwaffe aircraft during September, and was the highest scoring pilot of the battle. He had shot down 11 Germans in Poland and France – making 28 in total. He was killed in a crash at RAF Northolt. Another high-scoring pilot was shot down on the 10th, Pilot Officer R F T Doe of 238 Squadron. He baled out wounded near Poole. He had 15 victories.

Over the next few days Me 109s continued to try, and often succeeded, in penetrating to London where they dropped their bombs in random fashion. RAF fighters continued to climb up and engage these raiders but often combat claims of both sides were more or less even. However, night raids were on the increase. The RAF had won the day battle but it was weak in night defense. Despite Britain's preoccupation with building a night-bomber force to use against Germany, it had badly neglected a night-defense plan. Antiaircraft fire was really the first line of defense. Apart from this the RAF struggled along with Blenheims, Defiants, Spitfires and Hurricanes, but the latter, despite some successes, were not designed for this role. One day fighter pilot described a night sortie as trying to locate a fly in the Albert Hall, in the dark, without airborne radar!

The day fighting continued throughout the month, Spitfires and Hurricanes and

Above: Squadron Leader Michael Robinson, DFC of 609 Squadron, AAF. *Top:* 'Stan' Turner of 242 Squadron, Coltishall in the summer of 1940. *Top right:* Messerschmitt Bf 109E, 'Red 13,' shot down over Sussex on 25 October. Its pilot was 'captured' by a local farmer. *Above right:* Spitfire pilot, 1940.

Above: Pilots of 46 Squadron at Stapleford Abbotts in October 1940 being debriefed after combat. From left: Ambrose, Young, Leggett, McGregor, Earp, Lefevre.

Messerschmitts tangling in the autumn sky. Pilot Officer A N C Weir of 145 Squadron wrote on 17 October:

'We generally get told to patrol at 15,000 feet below the Huns, who dive from the south straight out of the sun. Also, whatever we are told, we climb as high as we can, preferably inland first and then out to meet what is obviously fighters, though one has to go and make sure they are not bombers. I see no point in engaging 109s at 30,000 feet as they can do no harm up there.'

The 29 October brought the last big clash, with raids upon London and Southampton.

No 602 Squadron, having managed to gain a tactical advantage of height and position, found themselves above the Me 109s for a change. In company with 222 Squadron they dived on the Messerschmitts from behind. Flight Lieutenant C J Mount was leading the squadron and in the initial attack and the subsequent chase when the 109s turned tail, they claimed eight of the German fighters shot down for no loss. The day's losses were 19 German to seven British.

The 30 October saw more fighter-versus-fighter actions, but overall activity was much reduced and it was not until late morning that the first plots appeared on the

British radar screens. Ten RAF squadrons were on their patrol lines, and six sighted the raiding aircraft. Two Me 109s were shot down but 222 Squadron up from Hornchurch lost two pilots and a Spitfire was damaged. In the afternoon 130 Me 109s streamed in across the south coast, and some reached London. Half a dozen were shot down but the RAF lost four aircraft, and 602 Squadron who had scored so well the previous day lost two Spitfires. On the 31st air activity was practically nil. The Luftwaffe lost 325 aircraft during October. The RAF lost 100 pilots with a further 85 wounded. It had been indeed a dangerous sky.

Right: Hurricane P3886 of 601 Squadron, AAF being 'turned round' at Exeter, November 1940.

Below: Hurricanes of 615 Squadron, AAF get airborne from Northolt.

It was now evident to everyone that the battle was over. The raids were greatly reduced, the bombers were few and far between and with the coming of winter the Germans could no longer maintain an offensive in daylight. In any case they had been so badly mauled that they could not make an effective assault except by raiding at night.

The accepted casualty figures for the Battle of Britain, the first major battle fought solely in the air, and which officially lasted from 10 July to 31 October 1940 are:

Luftwaffe aircraft lost	..	..	1733
German aircrew lost	..	..	3089
RAF fighters lost	..	..	915
RAF aircrew lost	..	..	503

Claims by both sides were much exaggerated at the time, the RAF claimed to have shot down 2698 German aircraft, the Germans claimed 3058 Royal Air Force machines.

Undoubtedly the chief architect of the victory gained by Fighter Command was its Commander in Chief, Air Chief Marshal Hugh Dowding. His control was faultless. His foresight in designing and building his air-defense system saved Britain in its darkest hour. Laurels too must go to Air Vice-Marshal Keith Park who had so ably commanded 11 Group which daily took the brunt of the assault. He commanded his squadrons with remarkable insight and courage.

Despite the victory, there was little respite for the pilots of Fighter Command. November continued to see the fighters meeting in combat in the sky over southern England.

No 145 Squadron got themselves into a tight spot on 7 November near the Isle of Wight. On patrol they were surrounded by three large formations of Me 109s – totalling about 50. The Hurricane pilots were unable to engage or dive away without exposing themselves to attack but the Me 109s began to pick off the members of B Flight. Five were hit and sent down and one pilot, Pilot Officer A N C Weir, DFC, was killed.

Four days later came the famous action when the Italians raided in the locality of Harwich. Nos 17, 46 and 257 Squadrons were in the air. Flight Lieutenant H P Blatchford, leading 257 Squadron, gained fame by destoying one Fiat BR 20 bomber and probably a Fiat CR 42 fighter biplane which he hit with his propeller.

The Italians were to make only a few intrusions over England in 1940. Another raid occurred on 23 November. No 603 Squadron found them and gave the call that they had spotted the ancient-looking machines. Another squadron in the area asked where they could be found. Perhaps an indication of the vast numbers and caliber of the enemy the pilots of 603 Squadron had been used to engaging was their classic reply:

'Shan't tell you, we're only outnumbered three to one!'

Bottom left: Three WAAFs decorated with MMs during the battle of Britain.
Bottom center: Some of 257 Squadron's pilots at Martlesham Heath, after their successes against the Italian raids.
Bottom right: Italian Fiat BR20 bomber shot down by Pilot Officer P G Leggett of 46 Squadron on 11 November 1940, in Rendlesham Forest, Suffolk.

Below: Just three of the 3080 pilots involved in the defense of England in the high summer of 1940.

Left: Roof spotters watching the fires from Northcliffe House, London.
Above left: Flight Lieutenant John Dundas, DFC, of 609 Squadron, AAF whose 13th claimed victory was the Luftwaffe 53-victory ace, Helmut Wick, on 28 November 1940. Only seconds later Dundas was killed by Wick's wing man.
Right: Damage in the center of Coventry, 16 November 1940.
Top: Hurricanes of 85 Squadron, led by Squadron Leader Peter Townsend, DFC, patrol over England. The skies were relatively free of German aircraft by late 1940.

They shot down several of them. Before this, however, another veteran, Flying Officer M B Czernin, DFC, of 17 Squadron, was shot down. On the 17th he attacked a formation of Me 110s of EG210, hit one but was then shot down by the famed Adolf Galland. Count Czernin baled out successfully. Flight Lieutenant Blatchford, again leading 257 Squadron shot down an Me 109 on the same day after a bit of a chase. The Me 109 pilot shot down a Hurricane during the fight but Blatchford finally nailed him:

'He continued to dive and I followed behind and above. After 30 seconds when at about 1500 feet, he flattened out and I put the finishing touches on him. The EA did a cartwheel and the pilot was jettisoned into the sea, pilot and aircraft hitting the sea at the same time 30 yards apart.'

The dangers in the sky continued to the end of the month. On the 28th came the now famous action when Flight Lieutenant J C Dundas, DFC, was lost near the Isle of Wight after possibly shooting down one of the leading German pilots, Helmut Wick of JG2. Dundas died with the yell of victory on his lips. In the air too was 152 Squadron, which was attacked by Me 109s which screamed through their formation, shooting down veteran pilot Pilot Officer A R Watson who had flown all through the battle. He baled out but tore his parachute in doing so and fell to his death. Pilot Officer E S Marrs went after the yellow-nosed Me 109:

'I followed and caught it up about 10,000 feet at about 10 to 15 miles south of the Needles. I waited my time and closed to about 100 yards. EA was not turning or weaving at all and evidently did not suspect any pursuit. I gave a short burst from astern and slightly underneath and oil smothered over my windscreen. EA did a half roll and dived down. I broke away . . . and when I saw it again, pilot was floating down by parachute. EA machine was descending in flaming fragments, evidently exploded.'

Each summer we remember and recall with pride that summer of 1940 when a handful of gallant young men daily carried out feats of great valor above southern England. Many died in the battle, others were to die before the war finally ended nearly five years later. As we watch the fast jet fighter aircraft of today we know that the spirit which the 1940 pilots engendered then still lives on in the men who fly above us today. Churchill's famous 'Few' gave of their best then. Let us hope that the men of today never have to show the world again what an air war can mean, not just to them but to everyone.

APPENDIX

Luftwaffe aircrew casualties

Bomber crews	1,176
Stuka crews	85
Fighter-bomber crews	212
Fighter crews	171
Crewmen missing	1,445
	3,089

RAF fighter bases during the Battle of Britain, in Fighter Command's three main Fighter Groups.

(Names marked with an asterisk denote Sector Headquarters.)

10 Group HQ at Rudloe Manor, Box, Wiltshire.

Pembrey*	Bibury
Filton*	Colerne
Exeter	St Eval*
Roborough	Boscombe Down
Middle Wallop*	Aston Down
Warmwell	Sutton Bridge
	Hawarden

11 Group HQ at Hillingdon House, Uxbridge, Middx.

Debden*	Biggin Hill*
Castle Camps	Gravesend
Martlesham Heath	Redhill
North Weald*	Hawkinge
Stapleford	Lympne
Hornchurch*	Tangmere*
Rochford	Westhampnett
Manston	Ford
Kenley*	Northolt*
Croydon	Hendon
West Malling	

12 Group HQ at Watnall, Nottingham, Notts.

Duxford*	Speke
Coltishall*	Ringway
Wittering*	Church Fenton*
Digby*	Leconfield
Kirton-in-Lindsey*	Yeadon

Aircrew who took part in the Battle of Britain

	Total	Killed
British RAF personnel	2,384	398
Fleet Air Arm	57	9
Australians	21	13
New Zealanders	100	11
Canadians	87	20
South Africans	21	9
Rhodesians	2	—
Jamaicans	1	—
Irish	9	—
Americans	7	1
Poles	135	29
Czechs	85	8
Belgians	27	5
Israelis	1	—
French	12	—
	2,949	503

A 32 Squadron Hurricane taxies out from dispersal at the forward landing ground at Hawkinge, Kent on 31 July 1940.

Squadrons, flights and other units which took part in the Battle of Britain

Sqdn No	Aircraft				
1	Hurricane	87	Hurricane	263	Hurricane
1 RCAF	Hurricane	92	Spitfire	264	Defiant
3	Hurricane	111	Hurricane	266	Spitfire
17	Hurricane	141	Defiant	302	Hurricane
19	Spitfire	145	Hurricane	303	Hurricane
23	Blenheim	151	Hurricane	310	Hurricane
25	Blenheim	152	Spitfire	312	Hurricane
29	Blenheim	213	Hurricane	501	Hurricane
32	Hurricane	219	Blenheim	504	Hurricane
41	Spitfire	222	Spitfire	600	Blenheim
43	Hurricane	229	Hurricane	601	Hurricane
46	Hurricane	232	Hurricane	602	Spitfire
54	Spitfire	234	Spitfire	603	Spitfire
56	Hurricane	235	Blenheim	604	Blenheim
64	Spitfire	236	Blenheim	605	Hurricane
65	Spitfire	238	Hurricane	607	Hurricane
66	Spitfire	242	Hurricane	609	Spitfire
72	Spitfire	245	Hurricane	610	Spitfire
73	Hurricane	247	Gladiator	611	Spitfire
74	Spitfire	248	Blenheim	615	Hurricane
79	Hurricane	249	Hurricane	616	Spitfire
85	Hurricane	253	Hurricane	421 Flight	Hurricane
		257	Hurricane	F.I.U.	Blenheim

Main Luftwaffe units which took part in the Battle of Britain.

Kampfgeschwader 1	Heinkel 111 and Dornier 17
Kampfgeschwader 2	Dornier 17
Kampfgeschwader 3	Dornier 17
Kampfgeschwader 4	Heinkel 111 and Junkers 88
Kampfgeschwader 26	Heinkel 111
Kampfgeschwader 27	Heinkel 111
Kampfgeschwader 30	Junkers 88
Kampfgeschwader 51	Junkers 88
Kampfgeschwader 53	Heinkel 111
Kampfgeschwader 54	Junkers 88
Kampfgeschwader 55	Heinkel 111
Kampfgeschwader 76	Dornier 17
Kampfgeschwader 77	Junkers 88
Lehrgeschwader 1	Junkers 88, Junkers 87 and Messerschmitt 110
Lehrgeschwader 2	Messerschmitt 109 and 110
Stukageschwader 1	Junkers 87
Stukageschwader 2	Junkers 87
Stukageschwader 3	Junkers 87
Stukageschwader 51	Junkers 87
Stukageschwader 77	Junkers 87
Zerstörergeschwader 2	Messerschmitt 110
Zerstörergeschwader 26	Messerschmitt 110
Zerstörergeschwader 76	Messerschmitt 110
Erprobungsgruppe 210	Messerschmitt 110 and 109
Jagdgeschwader 2	Messerschmitt 109
Jagdgeschwader 3	Messerschmitt 109
Jagdgeschwader 26	Messerschmitt 109
Jagdgeschwader 27	Messerschmitt 109
Jagdgeschwader 51	Messerschmitt 109
Jagdgeschwader 52	Messerschmitt 109
Jagdgeschwader 53	Messerschmitt 109
Jagdgeschwader 54	Messerschmitt 109
Jagdgeschwader 77	Messerschmitt 109

Plus various reconnaissance, air-sea-rescue, coastal and night intruder Groups.

INDEX

Acknowledgments

The author would like to thank the
following individuals who helped prepare
this book:

Jane Laslett, the editor
Adrian Hodgkins, the designer
Chaz Bowyer for supplying the pictures
 and writing the captions
Richard Natkiel for supplying the maps
Penny Murphy for preparing the index

Picture Credits

The author would like to thank the individuals and
agencies listed below for the use of their photographs
and artwork:
AELR Museum, Brussels: pp 8 (center), 40 (bottom
left)
Archiv Schliephake: pp 8 (top), 22, 51 (top)
Associated Press: p 16 (top)
R Athey: pp 2–3, 7 (top), 10 (top), 11, 14 (top), 34,
46–47, 60–61
Beaumont Aviation: pp 12 (top right), 13 (top),
15 (top)
BIPPA: p 19 (top)
Bison: pp 7 (bottom), 38, 42, (bottom), 49 (bottom
right), 53 (bottom), 58 (bottom)
CB Collection: pp 13 (center), 14 (bottom),
15 (bottom), 18, 19 (center right), 23 (center and
bottom), 24 (bottom), 25 (bottom), 26 (top right),
28 (top left), 29 (center right), 30 (bottom),
32 (all four), 36 (center), 37 (top left and top right),
41 (top), 43 (top), 45 (bottom), 48 (top), 49 (top
right), 50, 52 (top three), 53 (top), 55 (top and
bottom left), 56 (bottom left and right)
J B Cynk: pp 44 (top), 48 (bottom), 49 (top left),
54 (top)
Via H L R Franks: pp 19 (center left), 29 (center left)
Grp Capt C F Gray: pp 10 (bottom), 35 (top center)
Robert Hunt: pp 16 (bottom), 41 (center), 51 (bottom)
Imperial War Museum: pp 8 (bottom), 9, 12 (top
left), 13 (bottom), 17 (bottom), 18 (bottom), 20–21
(all three). 23 (top), 24 (top), 26 (bottom), 31 (top),
35 (top left, top right and bottom), 37 (top right),
43 (bottom), 45 (top and center), 52 (bottom),
54 (bottom), 56 (top), 57 (top), 58 (center left and
right), 59 (bottom)
P G Leggett: 55 (bottom right), 57 (bottom)
MOD (Air): p 56 (center)
C Order: p 29 (top)
PNA: p 33
Public Archives of Canada: pp 37 (bottom),
44 (bottom)
J K Ross: p 17 (top)
M Sargant: pp 29 (bottom), 39 (top left)
courtesy 32 Squadron: p 25 (top)
courtesy 56 Squadron: p 10 (center)
courtesy 74 Squadron: pp 26 (top left), 28 (top right),
30 (top)
R F Watson: p 4–5